THE WOMANLY ART
OF SELF-DEFENSE

THE WOMANLY ART OF SELF-DEFENSE

A Commonsense Approach

by Kathleen Keefe Burg

A & W Visual Library
New York

Thank you
My husband, David
My parents, Mr. & Mrs. Doyle O'Kelley
My editor, Muriel Bunge
My child, Jenny
My parrot, ding-a-ling

Published by
A & W Publishers, Inc.
95 Madison Avenue
New York, New York 10016

Library of Congress Cataloging in Publication Data

Burg, Kathleen Keefe.
  The womanly art of self-defense.

1. Self-defense for women.   I. Title.
GV1111.5.B87   796.8'1   78-71037
ISBN 0-89104-131-1
ISBN 0-89104-120-6 pbk.

Printed in the United States of America

Contents

1

SELF-DEFENSE: A COMMONSENSE APPROACH

There's a short cut to the parking lot down fifty feet of alley. You know you should never do this sort of thing, but you're fifteen minutes late for a date. You hurry down the alley. Suddenly you hear the sound of footsteps coming up behind you . . .

You're on your way up the stairs to your apartment, but you have an uneasy feeling. Is that someone standing in the shadows over there? Suddenly a hand reaches out and clamps over your mouth . . .

It's late at night and you're alone in your car. Suddenly you notice that a lone male driver is following you. You're miles from home, and the streets are deserted . . .

Can't happen to you? Well, don't you believe it! Violent crimes—from purse snatchings and muggings to beatings, rapes, and other brutal assaults—happen every day. And they happen to women.

These crimes often result not only in physical injury but also in severe psychological damage. In

9

many cases, one wonders why the victims of such crimes didn't try to defend themselves. Often the sad reply is that they never tried to learn how, perhaps because they believed "It can't happen to me."

This might sound frightening—and it is. Let's face it, we don't live in an ideal society. Terrible things *can* happen—even to you. But that doesn't mean you should lock the door and pull the covers over your head. If you have a healthy respect for yourself and your safety, you can and *should* learn to protect yourself. You have the right to feel safe wherever you happen or want to be.

I know I don't have to convince you any further that women today need to be able to defend themselves. If you read the papers and watch TV, you are already well aware of this fact. But the big question is *How do you do it?*

Well, let me assure you right off that to defend yourself successfully, you don't have to go in for intensive (and costly) training in the martial arts. Karate, for example, although highly effective, is not practical for most women. It is best left to the athlete who is interested not only in defending herself but also in learning a highly disciplined, competitive sport. To be a good student of this art, you must be in top-notch physical condition. Learning karate means long hours of practice and concentration. In fact, it takes years of study to become really proficient. Not exactly what you'd call a quickie course! Sure, a woman can sign up for a ten-week course in karate; but at the end of that time, she can't expect to march out onto the street ready to toss a six-foot, 200-pound man over her shoulder. She may have the knowledge and even the ability to do it, but her lack of experience and her insufficient practice could spell disaster if she tried.

Self-Defense: A Commonsense Approach

From my experience as a teacher, I've learned that most women are *not* interested in becoming female versions of Bruce Lee. What they *do* want is a logical, practical, and effective way to protect themselves without getting involved in expensive and time-consuming disciplines. And that's exactly what *The Womanly Art of Self-Defense* is all about.

What is the Womanly Art of Self-Defense?

To learn this method, you don't have to have the strength of an Amazon or the speed of Mercury. Of course, it's best to be in good physical condition under any circumstances; but it is not imperative for successful self-defense. My method is based on the use of *common sense* and the *natural weapons* that every woman has at hand, whatever her size, shape, or age. They are defenses that cost virtually nothing to learn and require little outside aid to develop. What are these mysterious "natural" weapons that every woman possesses? They are the normal human instinct of self-preservation—used with *control*.

It's a well-known fact that everyone harbors an aggressive instinct. This instinct is naturally aroused by any threat to our physical safety. Usually, because of the way girls are brought up in our society, women tend to suppress or deny the aggressive instinct. For example, many women tell me that they "couldn't hurt a fly." They think they could never build up the nerve or produce the "unladylike" behavior that it takes to protect themselves in time of danger. Well, to put it bluntly, that is the wrong way to think. Every normal person has—or can develop—the ability to defend herself when threat-

Self-Defense: A Commonsense Approach

ened with violence. Wherever you stand on the scale from militant "Women's Libber" to "Total Woman," you can still be aggressive in certain appropriate areas and at the same time maintain your own self-defined degree of femininity.

But the best thing about the womanly approach to self-defense is that if you apply the lessons taught here, you may never have to fight aggressively at all. That's because in this system, "flight" comes before "fight." In other words, the idea is to *prevent* any physical encounter by avoidance, escape, or other commonsense means.

Commonsense Rules of Self-Defense

These principles are what I call the commonsense rules of self-defense:

1. *Make every effort to avoid becoming involved in a dangerous situation.* For example, if you have the choice of walking ten blocks in a well-lighted area or half a block in a dimly lit alleyway, by all means walk the ten blocks!
2. If you are confronted, then do what comes naturally: *scream* bloody murder and *run* like mad!
3. If you cannot run away, then use some other nonviolent device that will *discourage your assailant.* Create a distraction, act, bluff, talk your way out of it—anything to get your body out of the danger zone! Even friendly persuasion works sometimes. Remember that the last thing an attacker wants is to lose face. Don't enrage him by suggesting that he is not capable of completing what he originally planned. Playing the role of a toughie or a heroine is strictly for the movies. In real life, don't play around with a man's pride (or anyone's pride, for that matter).

4. If all else fails, be prepared to *use physical techniques to prevent the assault* and enable you to escape.

The first three rules will be the easiest to learn—by reading and studying this book, thinking about the ideas, and applying them to your own life-style. For rule number 4, you will need to practice some basic physical moves. Of course, it will take some time to get to the point where you can perform the moves with the necessary agility, speed, and timing. But I have simplified and clarified the classic self-defense techniques so that you can prepare yourself against attack more easily and more quickly than with most other methods. And while you are learning the moves, you will be developing self-confidence, alertness, and the ability to stay relatively calm and cool if and when you need to put the moves into action.

The best way to learn this method is first to read this book through from beginning to end. Put it down for a few days, then pick it up again and start practicing some of the techniques in the first five chapters. Chapters 6 and 7 cover material that ideally you should be practicing all the time.

Learning and retaining the ideas presented here are very easy when you follow these steps:

1. Learn: Read this book through.
2. Understand and absorb: Reread this book.
3. Interpret: Apply the ideas to your own life-style.
4. Store: Give your thoughts time to settle.
5. Recall: This will happen automatically if you follow the first four steps.

Instant recall is what you need to develop. Obviously you can't stop and look up a certain section

Self-Defense: A Commonsense Approach

in this book in the middle of an assault. On the other hand, you can't study every day before venturing out to meet a friend for lunch or to take a stroll down Main Street. Learn the relaxed way, and your retention will be far greater.

Know Your Enemy

Since the concept of womanly self-defense centers on the ability to respond to an attempted assault *before* it can be completed, you must be able to recognize certain characteristics of an attacker. I have divided attackers into four main types and have given them nicknames.

THE PEST

This person will bother you simply because he is a nuisance; often he does not really mean any harm. He likes to "nudge" you until you get to the point where you might lose your temper. This type of annoyance can be recognized by the playful tone, and a mere push or slap on the arm, along with a smile on your face, will usually rid you of a Pest. Smiling is not quite enough, however, for you must establish direct eye contact to show him that you mean business. If the slap on the arm is ignored, try slapping a little harder until the person finally gets the picture. You will meet Pests in many social situations. They feel they have to bother someone to attract attention. The best thing is to try to avoid them. If you see a Pest approaching when you walk into a room, try a detour. If that is impossible, try to beat him to the draw by jumping in with a statement that will attract the attention of others. For example, you might say in a joking tone: "Well, look who's coming. The biggest pest I know! Who are you going to pester tonight? I'm too busy, and anyway I have my own personal bodyguard. Goodbye!" Then smile confidently as you stroll away toward others in the room. This method should throw him off guard.

The Pest may also turn out to be a little drunk in which case you follow these steps:

1. Keep him at a safe distance.
2. Turn and face him directly.
3. Reach out with your arms as if you are going to hold or caress his face in a loving manner.
4. Place your thumbs alongside his neck and dig down into his flesh.
5. Speak in a low but commanding tone and keep applying pressure until your point is well understood.
6. Quickly turn and quietly walk away.

THE ANNOYER

The Annoyer doesn't usually intend physical harm, but because of his own insecurities he attempts to annoy you with his sarcastic remarks.

I usually try to be extremely charming, for this will spoil his game and he will stop long enough for me to make a clean exit. Even if I become involved in a discussion with an Annoyer in front of a group, so that I am really put on the spot, all I have to do to control the situation is to agree with any statement the Annoyer chooses to make. Agreeing and smiling in a charming way will frustrate him and put a damper on his whole routine.

THE GRABBER

The Grabber is the aggressive type who comes on very strong, to the point where he is grabbing you and actually causing slight pain. This guy means business but may be somewhat hesitant about mounting a direct attack. If your sixth sense warns you about him, then by all means heed the warning. He is the type to wait for you secretly in the parking lot, under cover of darkness. The Grabbers of this world not only plan their assaults in advance—they also know their victims.

If you can't manage to stay in the company of someone who cares for your safety, then leave as soon as the Grabber starts to make advances. The longer you remain in his company, the greater the danger you are in. Remember, this is the type who will go out of his way to cause difficulty, so detouring this person and still staying in his vicinity will not solve anything. But before you leave, inform someone of the problem and ask to be escorted to your car or even all the way home. If you can't find help, then immediately telephone the proper authorities.

This is no time for heroics. Do not leave quietly and alone. The Grabber has already given notice of his intentions of inflicting harm. Heed the warning!

THE SERIOUS HARMER

This type is out to inflict harm in no uncertain terms. The Serious Harmer is also the kind who will attack you on the street for whatever purpose he has in mind. He doesn't even need darkness, but will be bold enough to attack in broad daylight.

Again, if your intuition relays a message of trouble, heed the warning and react! Inform someone of the problem and leave the vicinity immediately. The sooner you are out of the area, the better. And, I might add, it is better still to be accompanied!

Friendly Persuasion

Sometimes a totally different tactic works. Have you

ever been nice to someone who is about to tell you off? Your would-be opponent might end up apologizing for his behavior. Here are a few commonsense suggestions:

1. Smile when the attacker is solemn (this will surprise him).
2. The attacker who shouts is the attacker to whom you speak extra softly. The contrast may make him realize how idiotic he is being and often has a calming effect.
3. Courses in public speaking always teach you to take charge, be assertive, and look your listener straight in the eye. The same technique may also be used here to force someone into thinking twice about attacking you. No one will attack you if he feels that you are stronger and may defeat him, or even that you will fight back and cause him harm.

Distractions

Distractions are very good devices to use when confronted by an attacker.

1. Throw whatever you are carrying into the assailant's face. Then *run!*
2. Motion to an imaginary someone behind your attacker by nodding your head and calling to the invisible person for help.
3. Look quickly away, then back to your attacker. This might give you the split second needed for a self-defense maneuver. It's the old technique of faking and throwing your attacker off guard.
4. If you feel brave, you can pretend to attack and halfway through the attack withdraw, moving into a different position. This might throw your attacker off balance, giving you the chance to use another technique or run for help.

Self-Defense: A Commonsense Approach

Acting Skills

Suppose you are confronted with a serious situation and there seems to be little chance of getting out unscathed. Assume that in this case physical techniques won't work. Your best bet is to use your acting skills. After all, everyone has a little natural acting ability.

I can tell you about one act that was used successfully. A young woman who found herself in a tight spot went into an act of hysteria. She started screaming as if she were in pain. Her attackers were frightened off because of all the attention she was attracting. Her act went over where it counted, and she didn't mind getting a few curious stares from people nearby. She had saved herself from a worse fate.

A far more serious case occurred some years ago. Remember Richard Speck? He brutally assaulted eight nurses. Seven of them ended up as homicide statistics, but one nurse escaped death. The reason she escaped is that she lay completely still under a bed and pretended to be dead. After many hours, she finally ventured out—to safety. If she had panicked and tried to make a break for it, she would probably have wound up as another corpse. Acting saved her life.

I discuss a couple of my own favorite acts later, in Chapter 6 ("When the Doorbell Rings").

Controlled Anger

Any blatant attempt to hurt you physically should make you extremely angry. This anger is not only a

perfectly normal reaction, but also a valuable tool—
when used with *control*. Anger stimulates the adrenal glands, which in turn secrete hormones to excite
and heighten your emotional state. The hormones
also increase your physical strength so that you can
perform with that extra bit of zip. Did you ever feel
a tingling sensation before competing in some kind
of sports competition? This is the familiar butter-
flies-in-the-stomach sensation, and it means that
your body is sending you a signal: Help is on the
way. The body is a marvelous instrument that automatically "knows" how to help you in a moment of
stress.

But your body's automatic responses are not
enough to get you out of your predicament. Your
mind has to be working, too. If you don't lose your
head, you will be able to remember, and act on, these
basic instructions:
• Try to understand the situation logically.
• Think rationally about a plan of escape (if escape
  is possible).
• React with speed.
• Have the necessary timing when the assailant
  strikes.

Remaining calm and logical in a threatening situation is not always as hard as it sounds—especially
if you are prepared. Many people have found that at
the crucial moment they were not overcome by fear
and trembling but instead could act rationally and
effectively. (It's usually later on, when you are safe,
that you are overwhelmed at what *might* have happened to you!) So have faith in yourself. If you study
this method properly, you will have the knowledge
and the practice to react with confidence.

Practicing Your Moves

Once you're ready to start practicing the moves in Chapters 3–5, I suggest that you find a partner who is also interested in learning to defend herself. This will not only make your practice more fun, but may also be helpful in keeping you to the discipline you need in order to learn even this very easy system of self-defense. You and your partner can also exchange ideas. Talk out possibilities and act them out. Role-play is important.

Of course, it would be most helpful if you could find a man to help you practice on a real male body (after all, if you are ever attacked, your assailant is most likely to be a man). This might be difficult, though. I remember the reaction of some of my male friends when I told them I was writing a book on self-defense for women. They laughed nervously and pretended to be afraid that I would flip them over my shoulder and then give them a hearty kick you-know-where. You might meet with this sort of resistance if you ask a man to help you practice. But if you can enlist the cooperation of your husband or an understanding friend or relative, by all means do so.

Whether you practice with a man or a woman, it is important that your partner react naturally so that you will know what to expect in an actual combat situation. For example, if you kick toward the groin, your partner should double over. Or, if you smash your head backward into your partner's face (remember, this is only practice, so don't really smash!), your partner should loosen her hold on you and clutch her face as if in pain.

With your partner, practice a few of your favorite techniques in slow motion. This will help you find out if your techniques work and what adjustments you might have to make to improve them. Also practice situations in which your technique fails and you must quickly plan your next move.

PRACTICING ATTIRE

When you first begin to practice your kicks, strikes, and blocks, wear comfortable garments. A warm-up suit or leotard and tights are best. After a while, when you become more proficient, start practicing in your normal everyday attire. If you are ever assaulted (and I hope you never are), you will most likely be wearing everyday clothing, unless you happen to be on the tennis court or jogging through the park in a sweat suit at the time.

Depending on your particular taste in clothes, you may find that your everyday outfits impede free and easy movements. Your strikes might be hampered by a finely tailored jacket, or your kicks shortened because of a narrow skirt. You might even be thrown off balance by the clogs or high-heeled shoes you are wearing. It's a good idea to bear this in mind whenever you are dressing to go out somewhere where you might possibly run into trouble. Fashionable styles may be attractive and fun to wear—but it's a lot more fun to be alive and unharmed! In addition, some outfits may even provoke attacks. For example, I would never wear furs and diamonds in Chicago's Loop at night. To do so would be to advertise myself as a walking target for muggers. Similarly, strolling alone along New York's Central Park at night in hot pants and a sexy halter is hardly appropriate, for obvious reasons. Save that little outfit for where it belongs—on a nice crowded beach, for example, or in the privacy of your home.

CHOOSING YOUR TECHNIQUES

Unless you have a great amount of time to practice those techniques which require such application in order to build up the necessary speed, just try to select a few according to these criteria:

• Techniques that you feel confident with
• Techniques that give you a free-flowing action
• Techniques that make use of natural coordinated movements
• Techniques that protect the entire body

You cannot, for example, concentrate solely on kicking. What will happen if a situation arises where it is impossible to use your legs? Are you going to say to your attacker, "Wait a minute, stop and do it all over again because you grabbed me wrong and I can't use my kicks"? Ironically, there are instances in which you just might get away with this act; but the odds are heavily against it. An attacker is usually extremely nervous, and you are more likely to frighten him into doing something twice as dangerous as he had planned.

The example I just used might seem inconceivable, but the situation could arise where you will have to exercise your knowledge of blocking and striking—in other words, using only the upper part of the body. This means that what you are able to execute with the right side of the body, you must also be able to execute with the left.

Start by thinking of the body as a whole, and then draw a mental line down the middle, starting from the top of the head, dividing the body vertically into right and left sides. Of course, if you are right-handed like most people, all techniques will be easier on the right side. But, heed my warning, the left side is as vulnerable to attack as the right side. The odds are fifty-fifty as to which side you will be attacked on, so practice evenly. I have found from experience that I have to practice twice as much on my weaker side because of the lack of development there. If you are ambidextrous, great! You have a head start on most of us, for both sides of the body should work quite well.

Further tips on practicing and choosing your techniques are given at the end of Chapter 4.

2
SCREAM AND RUN!

Screaming

Screaming, which comes quite naturally in a moment of fear, is one of your most important defenses. Here's why:

1. The sound might alarm your assailant and make him abandon the attack.
2. Screaming and yelling as you kick and strike will add extra zip and spirit to your techniques. I would even venture to say that producing this noise will stimulate your adrenal glands, which will produce the substances your body needs to make that extra effort.
3. Screaming as you defend yourself will also discourage an attacker, showing him that you have the determination to ward off his assault. You are letting him know that he has picked on the wrong person, for you are going to give him a darn hard time in completing his attack.

4. Yelling can give you a certain emotional confidence. You are in effect expressing to yourself—as well as to your assailant—"I know what to do, how to do it, and dammit, that is exactly what I'm going to do!"
5. A loud scream will alert others to the assault, and someone may come to your aid. It might even be heard by police officers in the vicinity.

Unfortunately, it often happens that when people hear a scream, instead of coming to the rescue, they shy away to avoid becoming involved in any danger. They may just look in the other direction and completely ignore the cry for help. Or they may watch curiously from a distance. Some people will notify the authorities, giving the information under a false name to avoid involvement. Others may refuse even to answer the door when someone is knocking and calling for help.

Sad, isn't it? But this is the way our society has become. Sometimes you can't really blame the individual, for there have been many reports in which the "Good Samaritan" who runs to help a victim is injured or killed, is unjustly accused of the crime, or is threatened by associates of the criminal after he has been arrested.

It is not my purpose here to analyze the causes; I'll leave that to the sociologists. But I do want to make you aware of the fact that bystanders are not likely to come to your aid. Even if there's a telephone booth nearby, don't count on Superman to emerge—and Wonder Woman is probably all tied up elsewhere! So in most cases, you'll have to fend for yourself.

There is, however, a clever way to get help when you need it. Studies have shown that yelling

"FIRE!" does bring people quickly to the scene, whether out of curiosity or the excitement of watching the fire trucks arrive and the firefighters at work. Whatever the reasons for the "turnout," it might be a good idea to scream "FIRE!" instead of "HELP!"

Running

If it's good to scream, it's even better to run. And everyone knows how to run, right?

Wrong. Having taught gymnastics (exercises in which running is required) for years, I know that untrained women do not understand the proper technique of running. The typical untrained run is not as fast as it should or could be. One of the simple reasons is that most women lose speed when their arms fly out away from their bodies, causing them to sway from side to side (a movement sometimes called the "feminine wiggle"). Another readily observed fault is the knees knocking together and the heels flying up behind the body. Some people might consider this kind of running "cute" and "dainty," but that's not worth much when you're running for your life.

Here are the simple techniques of running. If you already know them, fine! You're all set in the running department.

RUNNING TECHNIQUES

1. Keep the elbows waist-high and in close to the body.
2. Remember to maintain a straight alignment. Do not let your arms swing your body from side to side. This will cause you to lose valuable speed

and may even lead to turning an ankle—just
what you don't need when you are trying to make
an escape. Think of picking apples off a tree when
you run. This will help keep the upper part of the
body from swaying.

3. Raise your knees and drive your legs down into
   the ground as forcefully as possible. This will give
   you added thrust, which will increase your speed.

4. Your legs must also maintain a straight alignment. Picture a narrow passage or a set of rail-
   road tracks and try to keep your body right down
   the middle, with the right leg on the right track
   and the left leg on the left track. The imaginary
   tracks should be shoulder-width apart.

5. Lean your body slightly forward. This will help

you use your body weight to increase momentum.

6. Breathe! Even though breathing is an involuntary reflex, some people unconsciously hold their breath when confronted with any type of stress. *Inhale* through the nose and *exhale* through the mouth. There are other systems of breathing, but I find this works best for me. Remember, the body needs oxygen to supply the needed amount of energy.

7. Keep your head up! If you drop your head forward as you are building up speed, you risk toppling forward head over heels. The position of your head is a major factor in controlling your body's balance. To test this, try dropping your head abruptly forward while running; you will sense a tendency to fall on your face. Reverse this action and throw your head back; you will feel your body falling in a backward direction. So head up!

8. Look in the direction you have chosen to run. Imagine if you were running from an attacker and you turned right into a brick wall—or even worse, into the arms of his accomplice!

9. Do not run either on your toes or on your heels. This will cause complications in both areas. The best foot position is running perfectly flat-footed. Place your whole foot down at one time. Remember, you have built-in shock absorbers to protect the jarred body parts.

If you happen to be wearing high-heeled shoes during an attack, kick them off as fast as you can.

RUNNING PRACTICE

In addition to knowing how to run, you should also know how to practice running so you can stay in proper shape.

Don't just jump out of bed in the morning, yawn a

few times, and start running a couple of miles! It is extremely important to have a good warm-up; otherwise you will be the ideal candidate for a muscle strain, pull, or tear. Ease into the program at a slow pace so that you will be giving your body a fair chance to perform effectively.

Overall body stretch. This means from the top of your head all the way down to the tips of your toes. (See "Morning Routine," Chapter 7.)

Slow, loose run. This exercise is like a simple jogging action in place. It should be performed similarly to the way a horse prances—nice and easy.
1. Lift the heel of the right foot without taking the toes off the floor.
2. Transfer all your weight to the front part of the foot.
3. Roll the foot down until the heel is once again resting on the floor.
4. Now do the same with the left foot.
5. While the lower part of your body is moving, shake out all the muscles in the hands, arms, neck, and shoulders.
6. As you do steps 1 through 5, start concentrating on your breathing:
Deep, slow inhaling through the nose for a count of five
Deep, slow exhaling through the mouth for a count of ten

Jumps
1. Stand with the feet pointing straight ahead, three to five inches apart.
2. Spring up into the air. The front part of the foot leaves the ground last, with the toes pointed.
3. Land with the knees and ankles slightly flexed.

The front portion of the foot lands first. (For ballet enthusiasts: The starting position is similar to first position without a turnout.)

Note that both feet leave the ground at the same time and return to the ground at the same time. Here are the important points to remember when executing jumps:
• Back straight
• Head erect
• Eyes forward
• Arms to the side
• Knees and ankles slightly flexed on landing

Practice jumping to a count of 1-and-2-and-3. Repeat three times.

Increasing momentum. Jog slowly and increase your momentum for one-half to two blocks, building up to full speed. Remember these points:
• Easy jog
• Mentally check body positions:
  Head
  Arms
  Elbows
  Hands
  Chest area
  Knees
  Legs
  Ankles
  Forward tilt of body

The distance you jog depends on your present physical condition. If you are just starting, I would suggest the bare minimum. After reaching your marked goal, do not stop abruptly but come to a slow, easy, *gradual* stop. Continue moving by walking. At the same time, concentrate on your breathing. *It is of utmost importance to continue moving.* If you are tired, the worst thing is to slump down to the ground and rest.

Take-offs. In an emergency, you are not going to be able to start running nice and slow and then build up to full speed. On the contrary, you will have to run at full speed from the start—almost instantaneously. But that's not what you do when you're just starting to get in shape. From a full upright position, practice taking off at a slow speed. Repeat and substitute medium speed. Repeat and substitute fast speed.
• Slow starts: 3 times
• Medium starts: 5 times
• Fast starts: 5 times

Sprints. A sprint is defined as a short race run at full speed. This is exactly what you need when you are making a speedy exit. Try to visualize mentally how far fifty yards is, and sprint that distance. Be sure to slow down gradually after you have reached your goal. *Breathe!* Rest for three minutes and then repeat three times.

Running attire. Now for a few tips about the proper attire for practicing your running techniques. No, they are not going to be exclusive *Vogue* magazine originals! Although I do like to look nice when practicing, I am also practical about what is best for my body. Since I am asking my body to perform for me, the least I can do is give it the proper equipment.

Many of my friends jog and play tennis without the support of a bra. Whether they like it or not, I am constantly telling them how bad it is for the body. As you run, you jostle not only internal body parts but also external body parts. Constant jarring of the body will lead to the breaking down of the muscle tissue that is needed to support certain areas. This constant pulling down of a muscle in one direction without building up the surrounding muscles will eventually lead to sagging breasts. No matter how tiny you may be, the wearing of a properly fitting bra is imperative.

Shoes are also important, especially since you'll probably be running on concrete pavement. Today there are numerous reports of foot problems that contemporary urban dwellers are suffering from. So be sure to get good recommended jogging shoes before you start your running practice. I know you are not likely to have your jogging shoes on at the time of a possible attack, but at least give your feet a break when training them.

3

BATTLE PLAN

Stand in Your Own Defense

The stance that places you in the proper position to respond to an attack is the old model's stance: one foot in front of the other at a right angle.

Your arms should be in the "Thinker" position: The arm on the side of the body that has the foot in front should be bent, with the fingers supporting the chin. The other arm can comfortably be crossed in front of the tummy, supporting the elbow of the other arm.

This is the best way to be ready. Once you're in this position, you can easily project the leg in front into the attacker's shin. At the same time, the bent arm may be extended outward as a strike or used as a block. The arm lying across the stomach may be brought back to maintain balance and used as a strike if needed.

Because of the female's relatively small frame, we women need all the help we can get, and throwing our weight into a strike will double the exerted force. Try hitting a pillow without throwing any weight into it, and then try striking the pillow with all your weight propelled forward. You will definitely see a difference.

It is very important not to be off balance or flying through the air when trying to ward off an attack. Stay in a solid position with your feet planted firmly on the ground. I am five feet, three inches and weigh 105 pounds, yet I can perform effectively and obtain the force needed in my strikes. When I coil my hand back in a striking position, that hand can be projected straight ahead toward my target. The hips should be thrust forward into the strike and then immediately pulled back into a square stance.

When everything is coordinated, I guarantee that you will have a force that will surprise you. Any action is easier when you know how to move and to use your weight properly. Think of the tennis serve or golf swing that appears supereasy and results in a 200-foot drive. In other words, throw your weight into whatever you are doing.

It is also extremely important to keep your knees slightly flexed. Straight, locked knees make it easy for your attacker to knock you off balance, and you might end up on the ground with the attacker on top of you. (Incidentally, there *is* an escape for that awful predicament on the ground, and I explain it later, in Chapter 5.)

Keeping the knees slightly bent will help you to:
• Establish a solid position
• Run faster and faster
• Take off in a run at a faster start
• Spring out of the way when attacked

If the knees are straight and locked, it is very easy for an attacker to:
• Knock you off your feet to the ground, enabling him to rape you, if that is his plan.
• Shove you, perhaps by the shoulders, so that you will tip slightly backward and lose your balance, ending up in a defensive instead of an offensive position.
• Apply pressure that would result in a broken knee cap. (It takes only about seven pounds of pressure applied to a straight knee to cause a break.)

GET READY

If your sixth sense tells you someone is going to attack you, but you don't want to be obvious in case you are wrong, follow these simple suggestions:

1. Stand with your feet shoulder-width apart.
2. Keep your knees slightly bent. (This will increase your stability in case you *are* attacked.)
3. Relax as much as possible. The last thing you want to do is to appear tense.
4. Have your favorite (stronger) kicking leg slightly forward.
5. Try to maintain a weight distribution of 70 percent on your back leg and 30 percent on your front (kicking) leg.
6. Position your right hand as if you are holding your chin.
7. The left arm may be across the front of the body with the left hand supporting the right elbow. This stance will not telegraph to your prospective assailant that you are ready for this attack. But the great thing about this posture is that you *are* ready just in case anything does happen.
8. Finally, remember to keep your eyes constantly focused on your would-be attacker. Never, never, never take your eyes off him for a single moment. It is possible to focus on someone without being accused of staring if you keep a slight smile on your face. This smile might also help you to keep somewhat relaxed so you don't react foolishly or too soon.

Okay, now you realize that you are going to be attacked no matter how much bluffing you do . . . so be ready.

Show your attacker that if he means business, so do you! "Come on, buddy, let's get this over with. I have far more important things to attend to than wasting my time on you." Believe it or not, saying this to yourself will give you confidence that you never thought you would have.

Your attacker just might take one look at you and turn around and run, for he might think he has bitten off more than he can chew. Remember that you do have a fifty-fifty chance to get out of this situation, and at this point, since you are the one with everything to lose, why not try your luck?

Assume a fighting stance:

1. Model's stance—right foot in front, the left foot behind (or vice versa, depending on which side you favor). Your feet will form a T.
2. Knees slightly bent.
3. Right hand (or left, if you are left-handed) coiled back in a fist in striking position.
4. Left hand (or right, if you are left-handed) held in front of the body to be used as a blocking device.

The reasons for this stance:

1. The front foot may be used both for kicking or keeping distance.
2. This position will help you maintain your necessary balance—whether you have to jump limberly to one side or execute a kick to a vulnerable spot.
3. The coiled-back hand will be ready to strike an intended target.
4. The front hand and arm will be ready to block a strike, a kick, or whatever.

Since karate is so popular and most people can easily recognize a stance, it is entirely possible that the would-be attacker may not consider your postural position a bluff. He might think you are an expert and that he might end up on the losing side of the battle. From past experience—my own and others'—I have found that using such a stance is very likely to discourage an attacker. Don't underestimate the importance of acting in the womanly art of self-defense. It's one of your basic tools, and an effective act just might save you the trouble of having to protect yourself with physical techniques.

Keep Your Distance

To respond appropriately to an attempted assault, you must quickly estimate the distance between yourself and your attacker. If I were about ten feet from my assailant, I would not choose striking actions, because these techniques require a closer range. If I were within a one-foot range, I would not select kicking techniques that could easily be blocked by my own body. The point is that you have to use common sense in your selection of techniques to use in your particular situation.

Here is an easy format to follow:

If your range is five feet or more (the minimum to try to maintain), then the wisest thing to do is select techniques that feature kicking.

If you find yourself from one to three feet from your attacker, use strikes, blocks, and knee techniques. A sure measure of this distance is that your arm when extended can reach your assailant's body. In an actual attack, of course, you won't attempt to measure. It is through practice that you will develop an accurate sense of how close you are to your attacker.

If you are unfortunate enough to be in a very close position—meaning that the attacker is holding some part of your body by brute strength—then the elbows, the heels, and the back of the head should be the next weapons to consider. As a matter of fact, they are the only weapons you can use in such a position, so don't hesitate. Just use them.

FAR RANGE (FIVE FEET OR MORE)

Use kicks to these areas:
- Groin
- Kneecap
- Kidney area
- Shin
- Face (if the attacker is bent over)

Note that kicks to the face are used *only* if the attacker is slumped over—bent in half. You do not have to perform a six-foot-high classy kick to the face as you see some of the actors in karate movies do. Be realistic, not showy!

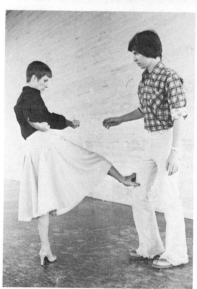

47
Battle Plan

MEDIUM RANGE (ONE TO THREE FEET)
Use strikes to these areas:
- Face (general)
- Ear
- Side of head
- Throat area
- Bridge of nose
- Groin

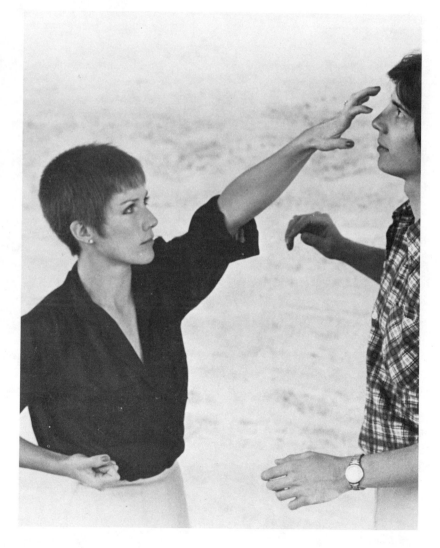

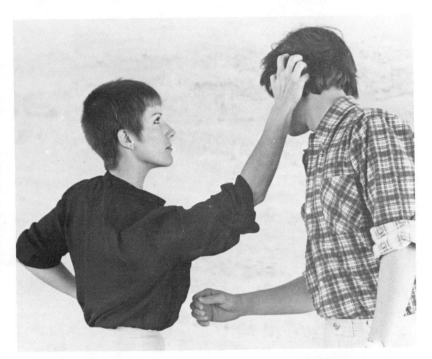

49
Battle Plan

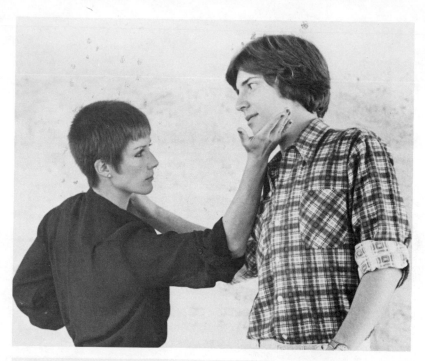

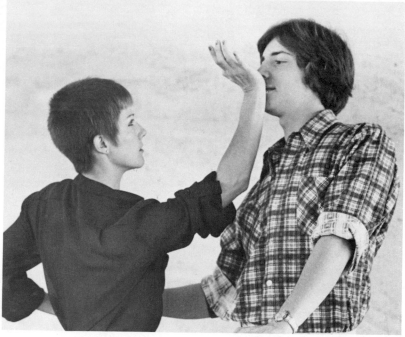

Battle Plan

Use blocks with your:
- Forearms
- Wrist
- Knee
- Fist
- Side edge of foot

Use the knees to strike these areas:
- Groin
- Face (if attacker is bent over)
- Kidney area (if you are behind attacker)

53
Battle Plan

CLOSE RANGE (HELD POSITIONS)
- Face (if attacker is behind you and is slightly bent over)
- Rib cage (same as above)
- Rib cage (if attacker is standing to your side)

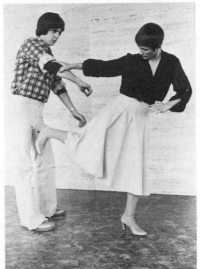

Use your heels in these ways:
- Stomp instep (when attacker is either to the side or behind you).
- Kick at groin (same as above).
- Kick at face (if attacker is bent over and your back is to him).

Use the back of your head to smash into the attacker's face when he is holding you from behind.

Below the Belt (and Other Vulnerable Spots)

The first thing to think about in a confrontation is how to get away as fast as possible. After realizing that the only way to do this successfully is to disable the attacker, you must proceed in accordance with the vulnerable areas of the human body. All the areas will be contacted differently depending on the distance that is being maintained.

THE SEVEN MAJOR AREAS (*See page 93*)

Eyes. If the attacker cannot see you, he will have a hard time trying to complete the assault. So if you're at a medium-range distance, the fingers on your dominant hand should be immediately split to a spread-open position and directed straight into the attacker's eyes. This should blind him temporarily and enable you to make your getaway. Or the pain may weaken him to the point where you can follow up with another technique. If one technique works, fine—let it go at that. You aren't there to show off all the clever techniques you've learned. Just do what is necessary and take off!

The typical reaction of an attacker when struck in the eyes is to cover the injured area with his hands and slightly double over by bending forward. When this happens, you can grab the back of his .head and push downward as your knee juts up right into his face. Then turn and run! And *breathe!* Otherwise you will lose the energy you need.

This is just one example of many techniques that can be successful in this situation. I used this one to start you on a thinking process, so that you will have in mind some sensible procedures and techniques that you can use when and if you are ever in that can't-happen-to-me situation.

Groin. The groin has been overemphasized in self-defense books as the perfect spot to contact in order to disable a male attacker. If the technique is not applied effectively, not only will you fail to disable him, but—because of the injury (not to mention the insult)—he may become so enraged that he will double his efforts and go after you with a vengeance. On the other hand, if you practice and develop a strong kick or knee action into the groin area and have

faith in your ability to deliver this type of technique, then by all means use it. However, do not further jeopardize your safety by provoking the anger of your attacker. Any technique you use must be performed 100 percent or not at all.

The type of contact made to the groin depends on your distance:

- Far range: kicks
- Medium range: knee action (You have to pull your attacker in toward you as you propel your knee forward.)
- Close range: fist, heel, or knee

Instep of foot. Probably at one time or another you've had someone accidentally tread on your instep. The extreme pain that resulted made you want to scream, but instead, you probably had to stand there and graciously accept the offender's apologies. Well, remember the pain—and that *you* can be the one to inflict it if necessary. A stomp on the instep can be extremely effective in a close-range position. This technique will usually loosen your attacker's hold and slightly weaken him.

Kneecap (patella). Professionals have stated that it takes only seven pounds of applied pressure to break a kneecap. The only problem is that the area is quite small and is not always the easiest spot to hit, especially when you are in a frightened state of mind. Because it is so small, great precision and concentration are needed to contact this spot successfully. In practice sessions, I've missed many times. And I found that in missing the target, I often received a mild injury on contacting the attacker's bone. So I always keep in mind that while the kneecap is indeed a vulnerable area, in an actual situation it is not one of my more successful areas of vulnerability. Of course, what doesn't work for me might work for you, and vice versa. So practice on this area until you can determine whether or not it is very easy for you to contact.

Windpipe (trachea). The windpipe may be disabled by using the blade side (little finger) of the hand, usually in a medium-range distance. The function of the windpipe is to accept air from the nasal area and transmit it to the rest of the body where it is converted to energy.

If you hit your attacker in this area, you will temporarily numb him, giving you the chance to turn and run. You will also cause him to weaken slightly, so that if you needed to, you could apply a knee to the groin and then follow up with a knee to the face as you pull his head downward. Sounds brutal, doesn't it? But would *you* rather be the one who is beaten, raped, and left lying in a gutter? Not me!

Bridge of nose. Very slight pressure applied to the bridge of the nose can greatly injure an attacker. In practice sessions, I often use this area in a follow-up or what can be called a secondary action. In other words, after your knee contacts the attacker's face (his head having been pushed downward), the nose is usually a natural target. Or, to cite another example, after your fingers have been applied to the attacker's eyes and he is slightly doubled over, the ridge area of the thumb may be used to strike upward underneath his nose. This technique is described in detail later on.

If you strike the top of the nose instead of underneath, you will cause bleeding, but don't let this frighten you. Better his blood than yours!

Kidney area. If somehow your attacker should have his back toward you (anything is possible in a scuffle), be sure to remember the good old-fashioned "kidney punch."

If you look at an anatomical model or illustration showing all the internal organs from the back, you will see how vulnerable the kidneys are. These two major organs have nothing to hide behind. They are not protected by skeletal bones or muscles, nor are they surrounded by other, less important organs.

To apply the kidney punch:
1. Grab the assailant's collar or some other part— hair, shirt, jacket—anything you can get a firm hold on. Do this with one hand.
2. With the other hand coiled back in the basic strike position, aim for your target. The success of

this strike depends on your putting all of your body weight into the attack. (Remember what I told you about how important it is to use your hips for an extra added thrust of power?) Any strike in the kidney area will cause superpain.

SECONDARY AREAS OF VULNERABILITY

Although the seven areas of the body listed in the preceding section are the ones to concentrate on, there are other possibilities. Don't overlook them.

Back of the knee. If you kick an attacker behind the knee, he will usually collapse.

Ankle. Kicking or stomping your attacker in the ankle will cause a certain degree of pain. But this area is so small (like the kneecap) that you really have to tune in your concentration if you hope to disable your attacker.

Face. Striking the temples, which are situated just above the ears on the sides of the head, may have these results:
• A light blow will stun.
• A medium blow could render one unconscious.
• A heavy blow is fatal.

To complete a strike in this area, you have to be in a medium- or close-range position.

Ear. The heel of the hand may be used to strike the ear. This causes pain, but not as much as in other areas you could be attacking instead of wasting your time here. But who knows what position or range you will be in when attacked? So anything goes. You should be prepared to strike any part you can, but don't waste your energy on areas where your strikes won't have an effect.

Neck. The blade side of the hand (where the little finger is located) may be used to strike the side of the neck. This strike, if delivered forcefully, will temporarily stop the flow of blood to the head. For extra force, try using two hands clasped together. This strike can be delivered to:

• Either side
• Front (Adam's apple)
• Back (usually when attacker is doubled over)

Rib cage. The elbow into the ribs will stun your attacker and possibly knock the wind out of him, giving you that split second to turn and run. But you must be very precise when striking this area as it is important to get at that last rib (sometimes called the floating rib).

I am often asked why I don't include the rib cage and the abdominal area among the major targets. The reason is quite simple, as you can prove for yourself. Ask a cooperative man—your husband, brother, or boyfriend—to let you strike him in the abdomen or the stomach. If he tightens his muscles, as an attacker would probably do instinctively, your striking him in these areas will hardly faze him (unless you have tremendous power). So why attack your attacker where he is strong and waste all your precious energy?

4
BASIC SELF-DEFENSE MOVES

67
Basic Self-Defense Moves

2. Throw the hips into the direction of the kick (this will help produce the desired power).
3. Keep one arm coiled at the side of the body, waist-high, while the other arm blocks the side of the body that is kicking.
4. After you've thrown the hips into the kick, recoil the leg and foot by returning the hips to a square position.

Practice the thrust kick to a count of 1-and-2 (rise, thrust, recoil).

For an effective kick of either type, the foot must be in the proper position:
• Foot slightly flexed
• Toes curled upward

(Note: Some other kicks have the foot in a point position, with the toes pointing downward. For these kicks, I will specify what position is required.)

Even if you always wanted to get into show biz, forget about trying to kick over your head like a Rockette. The high kicks you see performed on a chorus line are not realistic in the street situation. A kick aimed at the face of a six-foot man not only would be difficult, but would also take too long to complete. And what you're after is quick results. So it's important to know that you'll probably get better results by aiming at a lower target area—such as the groin—than by attempting a kick to the face.

STOMP KICK

This thrust kick is one of my best techniques for the simple reason that I can deliver it with force and at the same time use it as a block. Here's how to practice it with your partner:
1. Start by facing your partner.

2. If you're using the right foot to kick, pivot on your left foot to a 90-degree angle (right angle).
3. Draw and lift your right knee upward.
4. Extend the right side of the foot outward by straightening the leg.
5. Propel the heel forcefully toward your target. You will be kicking using the right side of the right foot, the side where the little toe is.
6. Contact your target (keep your concentration tuned in to your target).
7. Recoil your foot back to the knee-high position and replace it on the ground.

Now, you are worried about maintaining your balance? Don't be. As you extend your foot into the target, lean slightly away from the direction your foot is traveling. This will keep you in balance (with practice).

Body parts where this kick may be directed effectively are as follows:
• Knee (front, side, back)
• Shin
• Instep
• Outside of foot

The stomp kick may also be used as a blocking technique if someone tries to kick you.

KICK TO GROIN (MEDIUM RANGE)

1. Curl toes upward.
2. Lift knee.
3. Extend foot out from the knee joint.
4. Thrust or snap foot into attacker's groin.
5. Instantly recoil foot.
6. Replace foot on ground to reestablish a firm stance.

Basic Self-Defense Moves

KICK TO INSTEP (CLOSE RANGE)

1. Coil foot up by lifting knee.
2. Extend heel.
3. Straighten leg and smash it down into assailant's instep.
4. Lean backward slightly in order to maintain your balance. You will still get a lot of power out of this kick, and the last thing you want is to kick and fall toward your assailant where he could grab you.

Basic Self-Defense Moves

KICK TO SHIN
Same as above.

KICK TO SIDE OF KNEE
Same as above.

HEEL TO GROIN
Use this when you are being attacked from behind.
1. Lift knee.
2. Look over your shoulder at your assailant.
3. Propel heel backward into attacker's groin.
4. Keep the arm that is on the kicking side up as a block.
5. Keep the other arm coiled and ready to strike.

73
Basic Self-Defense Moves

SNAP TO FACE

Use this when your attacker is doubled over.
1. Lift knee.
2. Point your foot upward.
3. Snap your foot into his face.
4. Recoil quickly and return foot to ground.

DOUBLE POWER TO THE FACE

1. Jump into the air by lifting the left knee.
2. Switch legs in the air.
3. As feet exchange, the right foot contacts the assailant's face.

This technique delivers twice as much power, but it takes twice as long to deliver. Only if your assailant is doubled over and is quite immobile do I suggest using this technique. This is because I do not like the idea of flying through the air in order to execute a kick. If you have the energy and you want to make sure your assailant is really going to be incapable of pursuing you, then by all means

Double power to face

Knee into groin

use this! Even if you don't expect to use this technique, it's fun to practice.

KNEE INTO GROIN (CLOSE RANGE)
1. Lift knee.
2. Propel knee into groin.
3. Repeat until attacker is weakened and, if he has been holding on to you, his grip is released.

KICK TO BACK OF KNEE
1. Grab back of attacker's head (hair, collar, skin, etc.).
2. Pull his head backward.
3. Simultaneously with number 2, extend the blade side of your outer foot into the back of the knee. (This should make him collapse.)

RUNNING ATTACKER
Suppose an attacker is running toward you at full speed and you have no place to escape. In other

Basic Self-Defense Moves

words, you are cornered and have no choice but to defend yourself in some way.

1. Stay about twelve to fifteen feet from the wall or whatever obstacle is behind you. Try to give yourself as much room as possible.
2. Stand with your back toward the wall.
3. Brace yourself (feet are shoulder-width apart). Yes, this will take nerve—but what alternative do you have?
4. As the attacker runs toward you, reach out and grab him as he gets close to you.
5. Sit down at the same time, placing your foot right into the pit of his stomach.
6. Roll backward and extend your leg straight.

You will be using your attacker's momentum and his forward motion to propel him up and over your head, smashing into the wall. Honest! This *does* work, and you don't have to be strong and your timing doesn't have to be perfect. Many times, while practicing this technique, my timing was not the best, yet I still managed to execute it. And I always feel that I have really accomplished something. It's a good feeling to know you can be in complete control without exerting a great deal of effort.

POSITION OF UPPER BODY DURING KICKS

So far I have concentrated my instructions on how to use your lower body in kicking techniques. But keep in mind that the way you use the upper part of your body is also important. The same two rules apply to all of the techniques described above:

1. The arm on the same side as your kicking leg should be coiled back at the side, waist-high, ready to strike.

2. The other arm should be held high in a blocking position.

This position not only helps to maintain balance but prepares you to be able to easily step into your attacker with a follow-up strike. Sometimes a single kick or even a series of kicks is not sufficient to complete the disabling of your assailant. A kick to one area followed by a strike to another vulnerable body area is more effective.
EXAMPLE: Kick to the groin immediately followed by a strike to the eyes.
Sometimes this is more effective than the continuous kicking, for you may lose your balance after the third or fourth kick. Try and see what is easier for you . . . the continuous kicking or a kick followed immediately by a blow or strike.

Striking

BASIC STRIKE
The basic strike is as follows:
1. Coil the right hand (or left, if you are left-handed) at waist level, palm up.
2. Propel the blow straight out, turning the palm down.
3. Hold the arm, wrist, and hand in a firm position.
4. Use the flat part of the two large knuckles as the striking surface.

This strike can be delivered to any level:
• Eyes
• Temple
• Throat
• Chest

Basic Self-Defense Moves

Basic Self-Defense Moves

79
Basic Self-Defense Moves

- Pit of the stomach (solar plexus)
- Abdomen
- Kidneys
- Groin

The basic position of the striking hand is the *fist*. Clench your four fingers as tight as possible into the palm of your hand. This gives you the best striking surface—namely, the top of the knuckles.

OTHER STRIKES

Other possibilities are as follows.

Heel of hand. Using the heel, or butt, of your hand, you can effectively contact:
- Side of head
- Rib cage
- Under chin

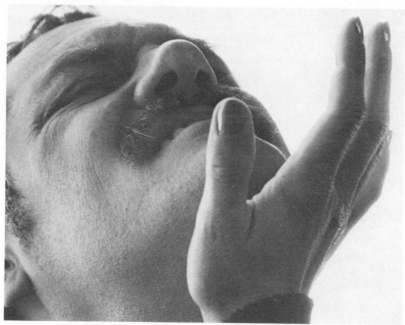

Heel of hand

Basic Self-Defense Moves

Split fingers

To execute:
1. Bend wrist slightly.
2. Spread fingers slightly.
3. Strike out with the heel of the hand.

Split fingers. Spread the fingers and use the tips. This hand position is primarily used against the assailant's eyes.

Back of hand. This is the fist position, but here you make contact with the flat part of the back of the hand instead of the knuckles. It can be used against:
• Face
• Side of head

Ridge of hand. Extend the fingers and bring them together to form a point. With the hand in this position you may contact:
• Throat
• Rib cage
• Kidneys

Hammer. With your hand in a fist, you use the flat section on the bottom. This is useful in contacting:
• Groin
• Side of face
• Top of nose

Elbow. This is useful when your attacker is trying to hold you. Aim your elbow against:
• Rib cage
• Face (when attacker is doubled over)
• Under chin

Elbow techniques are useful only at *close range* in a frontal attack, or in a rear attack.

Outside blade of hand. Keeping your striking hand straight and firm, cross the arm in front of your body. Propel the blade side of your hand into the throat area, using your hips to add extra thrust. Strike and then recoil.

The throat is your major target with this strike. Don't try to deliver a karate chop across the back of an assailant's neck, no matter how many times you've seen it in the movies! Unlike karate experts, most of us have very little muscle development in

Back of hand   Ridge of hand   Hammer

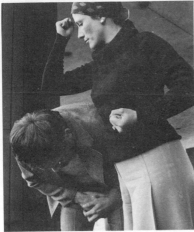

Elbow   Outside blade of hand

the blade of the hand. A better procedure for us ordinary folk is to use both hands when striking with this technique. Obviously, two hands will have twice the force of one hand. If your attacker is doubled over and you are standing to one side of him, clasp your hands together, extend your arms above your head, and with all your bodily might drive the blade side of the hands down across the back of his neck.

Blocking

There are three basic levels to consider when you

Basic Self-Defense Moves

are using any type of blocking technique: high, middle, and low. To get the picture, think of your body as being in a frame. That is the area you should block, never beyond. Otherwise you will be putting yourself in a position from which it will be difficult to recover. It will also take time to pull your block back into the center position in case your opponent decides to attack from another angle.

Don't open your body up to any attack your assailant may wish to use. What you want is to protect the important areas. It doesn't hurt so much to be hit on the arm or leg, but it does hurt and can do real damage if you are punched in the breast, face, or other vulnerable spot. So keep your arms in nice and close to the center of the body and hide behind your bodily fortress.

Now to some specifics.

TYPES OF BLOCKS

Forearm and crosshand. The high level is useful if the attacker happens to be approaching from above your head with a knife, stick, or simply a striking area.

The middle level can be used in order to block a club attack straight on. And it comes in handy when you not only want to block your assailant's weapon but also intend to grab the attacker in order to follow up with striking or kicking techniques.

The low level is useful in blocking a kick to the groin area.

Palm of hand. This is used when you do not want or need to resist too violently. For example, if a pesty character is trying to playfully caress you, just use the palm of the hand to push him away.

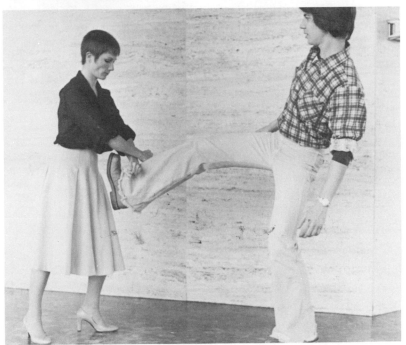

Basic Self-Defense Moves

Hammer. Use the flat side of the hand when it is in a fist position.

When you are using any of these blocks, be sure to protect the other areas of the body. Your attacker may be extremely fast, and once his move is blocked, he could spring back to attack you somewhere else. When one arm is blocking, the other arm should be ready to either strike or block once again. If the right hand is blocking, the left arm should be waist-high in a fist position ready to defend its territory. The parts of your body must work as a team. An attacker might set you up in a vulnerable position by faking a strike, and then jumping in and striking an exposed area with real power and force. Be ready for anything!

Blocking should almost always be used in combination with other maneuvers; for example: block, strike, kick; or block, kick, strike; or strike, block-and-kick together.

In the case of a surprise attack, the typical reaction is first to block and then kick or strike. If you know the attack is coming, however, it is good thinking to strike or kick as your attacker starts his motion. In this case, the use of a block might waste valuable time.

But since you can't know in advance what the battle plan will be, you must perfect your techniques. So be sure you are proficient on both sides.

Follow this exercise, using alternate sides:
• Block (right side)
• Strike (left side)
• Kick (right side)

Then reverse the procedure.

Here are some examples of a series of movements you will want to have at your command:

Basic Self-Defense Moves

A

1. Block middle level (left).
2. Split fingers to the eyes (right).
3. Palm up, strike under chin (left).
4. Grab both arms for balance.
5. Kick to groin (right).
6. Push away and *run!*

B

1. Block left-handed strike with right hand. At the same moment, spring to the left, with the right hand still blocking.
2. With heel of left hand, smash into the attacker's right ear or side of head.
3. Recoil.
4. Strike right hammer fist into groin.
5. *Run!*

C
(*See pages 88–89.*)
1. Block with the left hand; strike by springing to the left of your attacker.
2. Turn one quarter to the right.
3. Place your left arm on inside of attacker's right arm, below the elbow.
4. Place your right arm on outside of attacker's right arm, above the elbow.
5. Right arm moves straight toward your body; left arm moves in opposite direction away from your body. This simultaneous action should cause the elbow to snap. This is sometimes called an "elbow break," for good reason.
6. Step with the left foot to the left side.
7. Lift right knee and thrust the foot into the groin.
8. *Run!*

Basic Self-Defense Moves

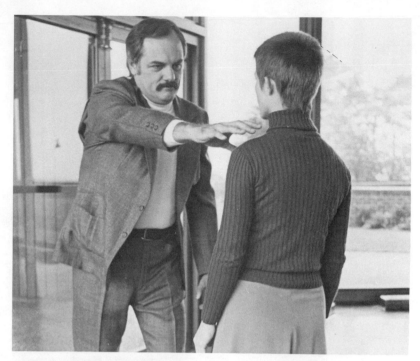

Basic Self-Defense Moves

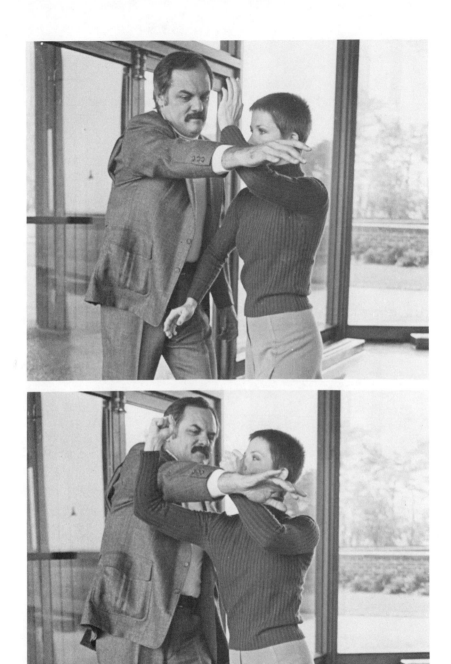

89
Basic Self-Defense Moves

D

The attacker is holding you from the front with both hands on your shoulders.

1. Place hands on each of the attacker's wrists.
2. Push down on his wrists, at the same time projecting your knee into the groin. (Remember to keep your eyes on your target.)
3. The attacker will likely bend over, clutching his injured groin. Immediately drop your arms to your sides.
4. Clasp your hands together and bring them thumb-side up into the attacker's nose.
5. Continue the action until your arms are above your head. This should throw the attacker backward with his arms up.
6. Turn and *run!*

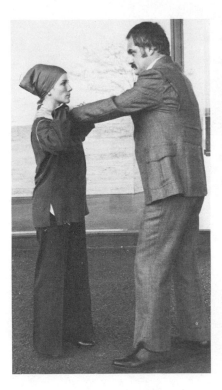

Basic Self-Defense Moves

Basic Self-Defense Moves

Practice Tips

Here are some tips to help you develop your self-defense moves without the aid of a partner.

First you need to picture your assailant. Buy a roll of paper and, with a felt-tip pen, draw a life-size picture of a villainous character and tape him up on the wall. Even better, tape a large sheet of paper to the wall and ask a male friend to stand against it and let you outline his body with a pencil. You will then have a realistically proportioned outline of a man's body. Go over the pencil lines with a marker and add a pair of mean-looking eyes. If you wish, draw X's or circles to mark the major vulnerable areas.

Now you're ready to begin. Face the picture of your attacker and practice some of the following moves.

KICKS

Be sure to calculate your distances by kicking from a stand, taking one step in, and varying your practice all the way up to three to five steps. Practice:
• 5 snap kicks to different parts of the body
• 5 thrust kicks

STRIKES

Practice all strikes aiming at different target areas. Be sure to emphasize thrusting the hips into every strike for extra power.

Build up your speed!

Concentrate on focusing your eyes on your intended target. Striking with your eyes focused on a different target will lessen your chance of hitting home.

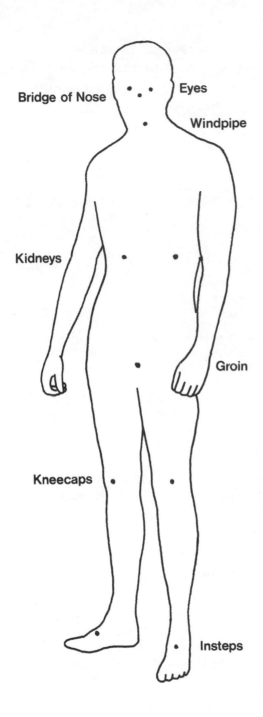

Bridge of Nose

Eyes

Windpipe

Kidneys

Groin

Kneecaps

Insteps

BLOCKS

At a close distance, be sure to practice all levels of blocks. Here you will have to imagine the different techniques your attacker is going to use against you.

COMBINATIONS

1. Kick.
2. Step in with a block.
3. Follow up with a definite strike.
4. Escape route—turn and *run!*

EXAMPLES

Think distances!

1. Far distance: Snap kick (right leg)
   Medium distance: Middle forearm block
   Close distance: Forward punch (right arm)
   Escape route: Turn left and *run!*
2. Medium distance: Forearm block
   Close distance: Split fingers to eyes (right hand)
   Escape route: Turn and *run!*

Think speed!

3. Block with forearm (jump to blocking arm side)
   Split fingers to eyes
   Grab and pull in as knee is jutted to groin
   Turn and *run!*
4. Block with right forearm
   Back of right fist to face
   Left forward punch to rib area
   Run!

I have given just a few examples. Now you must develop your own techniques—ones that work easily and successfully for *you.*

Once you understand distances and your reactions improve in speed, try to practice:

1. Blocking, *then* reacting
2. Blocking *and* reacting simultaneously
3. Reacting (You should be fast enough eventually to counteract a strike with a strike—don't become frustrated if this seems to take a long time; some self-defense experts still have problems with this stage.)

5
TAKE ACTION!

In a Tight Squeeze: Held Positions

In a "held position," the attacker is holding you so that it is nearly impossible for you to move. The assumption here is that your assailant does *not* have a weapon. Possible held positions, and how to cope with them, follow.

BEAR HUG (FRONT)

The attacker has both of his arms around you, trapping your arms in a tight grasp. Follow these steps:

1. Try to strike both of your hands into the sides of his body (a sharp jab).
2. Slam your knee into his shin.
3. When his hold is released slightly, you will have room to step back a little and propel your knee right up into his groin. Don't try to use the knee-to-groin while you are still in the tight hold, for you will be blocking your own knee and will not be able to inflict much pain.

99

4. If all else fails, use your head—literally! This might hurt you a bit, but you have no choice. Drop your head back slightly and jam the top of your forehead into his face. If the hold becomes tighter, then sink your teeth into the side of his neck. The old vampire routine! (I wasn't kidding when I told you that anything goes!)

BEAR HUG (BEHIND)

When someone grabs you from behind by wrapping his arms around your body and trapping your arms, then again you must use your head, but not to think with.

1. Drop your head forward, then fling it backward as hard as possible into your attacker's face.
2. Use your heel by kicking back and up into the groin area.

After these two moves, his hold should be considerably loosened, so you may follow up with another technique. For example:
• Elbow to face (attacker will be doubled over)
   or
• Elbow to the stomach area
• Last but not least—RUN! And don't stop to look back!

Take Action!

Note: The back (or crown) of the head is extremely hard and durable, so you will feel very little when using this area to smash into your attacker's face, but your attacker is going to be in painful trouble.

ATTACKER'S ARM AROUND YOUR SHOULDERS

A man walks up to you and puts his arm around your shoulders in what is obviously not a friendly gesture but a potential attack. He demands that you go somewhere with him, and he tightens his grip on your shoulder to prove that he means business.

Let's say that this person is at your left side, with his right hand holding on to your shoulders. Your moves should be as follows:

1. Tell him to leave you alone and try walking away.
2. If that doesn't work, place your weight on your right foot and pick up your left foot quickly straightening the leg and driving it down on your assailant's foot.
3. Next, jump slightly forward looking over your left shoulder at the attacker. When jumping, cup your right hand over your left fist and shove your elbow backwards sending it into his rib cage.

A typical reaction would be that he will double over, or at least bend forward slightly. He will also loosen his grip on your shoulder and be immobile for a few seconds. If, however, the attacker is still maintaining a hold, then you may have to do the following:
1. Drive your left fist into his groin.
2. Slam your left (or right) fist into his face.
3. Turn toward your attacker, who will be facing forward. You will then be facing his side.
4. Grab the back of his head and shove it downward as your knee comes up into his face.
5. Run—or, if the circumstances warrant it, walk away.

CHOKE HOLD (FRONT)

The attacker is facing you, with both of his hands gripped around your neck in a choking position.
1. Place your hands on the attacker's hands. This will help secure your balance.
2. Kick the groin.
3. Release his hands.
4. Drop your hands to your sides.
5. Clasp your hands together below your waist and fling your arms upward and outward with as much force as possible.

6. With your arms still above your head, clasp your hands again and come down as hard as possible onto the bridge of his nose.

7. Run.

CHOKE HOLD (BEHIND)

If you are being gripped around the throat from behind, there are two possible lines of action. Here is the first:

1. Lean your torso slightly to one side to clear your body out of the way. This is so that you won't block your own strikes by getting in the way.

2. Thrust your right hand back in a fist position directly into the attacker's groin. If this is done with force, his grip will easily be loosened.

3. Propel your right elbow into his rib cage, making him double over slightly.

4. Now slam your right elbow into his face. Steps 1 and 2 should have placed your attacker in a slightly bent-over position. (This action must be performed with great speed.)

And here is the second:

1. Hold on to your attacker's hands and dig your fingernails into his skin. Don't be afraid to draw blood.
2. Kick your heel into his shin.
3. Stomp down onto the attacker's foot with your heel. Repeat steps 2 and 3 until you feel his grip is starting to loosen.
4. Drop down slightly by bending your knees and leaning slightly from the waist.
5. Turn and clasp your hands together in a fist position and jam straight into his groin.
6. Run!

A third technique that I have been taught is one I would be reluctant to use. It consists of holding both of your attacker's hands and then dropping down onto the ground in a sitting position. This should release the attacker's grip, at which point you would turn, roll onto your feet, and run.

What bothers me is the idea of winding up on the ground. The risk is that if this technique is not completed properly, you are in essence helping the attacker! Different techniques work for different people. Therefore, you must be your own judge of what works for you and what the consequences might be if something goes wrong. The smart thing—and I can't emphasize this too much—is to *practice,* to know what you can do and thus to be prepared!

ATTACKER'S WHOLE ARM AROUND YOUR CHEST

You've probably seen one of those movies in which the hero, finding himself in this predicament, grabs the villain's head and flips him over. The villain goes flying through the air and ends up unconscious on the ground. Great in the movies! Forget it in real life. Instead, follow these steps:

1. Kick backward into his shin.
2. Propel your elbow into the middle of his body.
3. At the same time, try bending your knees to drop your weight down a few inches; also, tuck your chin downward.
4. Run!

The first three steps should definitely loosen the attacker's hold. But it's a good plan to repeat the kick to the shin and the elbow to the rib cage until you obtain results.

Here's another series of actions to be used in this situation.

1. Place your left hand on the attacker's left arm.
2. Step forward with your right foot.

Take Action!

3. Turn into the attacker's left arm on the left side (this should loosen a hold on your bent right arm that is being held behind your back).
4. Spin around to the left until you are facing your attacker.
5. As you spin, bring your right arm up next to your side and smash straight into the attacker's face. Do not let your arm go out and circle before striking, as this would telegraph your intention.
6. Kick with your left foot into the groin. If this doesn't do the job and your attacker is half bent over, then bring your foot up and kick his face.
7. Run!

LEGS GRABBED
(WRESTLING OR GRAPPLING)

Imagine that somehow or other you find yourself on the ground, either on all fours or flat on your back. Your attacker is either standing over you or on the ground trying to roll on top of you. This is a really serious situation, because once you are on the ground, there are very few defensive moves you can make.

Karate experts usually refer to the only defense available to you from this position as "grappling." I do not recommend that any woman resort to this technique by choice. But there is the possibility that you have fallen to the ground and the attacker is trying to grab your legs in order to pin you down. I have to be frank and state that a man's strength and body weight will usually win out, once you are down. If you are in this position and he is bent on rape, I'm afraid that if you value your life, you might as well close your eyes and hope he gets it over with quickly. But, if your attacker does not have a strong hold on you, I most heartily suggest that you try squirming out of his grasp. (Don't forget that we are assuming the attacker has no weapon.) Once your legs are free, start kicking as frantically as possible, at the same time trying to inch yourself away. Keep on kicking and inching away until (you hope) you are out of range, so that you can jump up and *run*.

There are no rules governing this type of defense. As a matter of fact, there's no such thing as "fair play" when it comes to defending yourself. Clawing, scratching, and biting are all quite "legal." In other words, use whatever weapons you have.

REAR ATTACK

Any time you are about to be attacked from the rear (that is, you are not already being held), follow these rules:

1. If you feel the attacker approaching, turn immediately to face him.
2. Block. Usually middle block is best.
3. React, either with a kick or a strike.

You may have to use a combination of all three; for example:
• Block, kick, strike
• Block, kick, strike, kick
• Block, kick-and-strike, kick-and-strike

Use whatever you feel comfortable with at the moment. And at the first possible chance—you guessed it—*run!*

If the attacker grabs both your shoulders from behind:

1. Pick up your left knee, grab attacker's hands, and dig your fingernails into skin, while looking over left shoulder.
2. Raise left knee high while hanging onto attacker's hands to help maintain your balance as you dig your fingernails to inflict pain.
3. Project left heel down into attacker's foot (scream as you stomp your foot into the attacker's foot).

4. Turn around (left) to face your attacker.
5. Spread feet in order to increase your stance for better balance. Clasp both hands together and focus on your prospective target.

Two Against One: Multiple Attacks

Many assailants are braver when they have a few friends around to help. As the saying goes, "There's strength in numbers." And this strength is exactly what you have to be aware of when two or more assailants are trespassing onto your private property—that property being your body.

Let's look at a typical situation. You are walking down a street when someone grabs you and pulls you into an alley where his buddy is waiting to help out with the assault. The first thing to do if you are not being held, or you have managed to release the hold, is to keep a safe distance. At the same time, try to analyze the situation. Quickly ask yourself the following questions:

• How many attackers are there?
• Are they armed with any weapons?
• If they are armed, which of the attackers seems the most confident!
• How are they positioned? (In other words, where is each one standing in relation to you?)

This must be done instantly. You are in no position to waste time. Above all, *keep your distance!*

Suppose you are the victim of a two-man attack, as diagramed here:

ATTACKER   ATTACKER

VICTIM
(YOU)

Take Action!

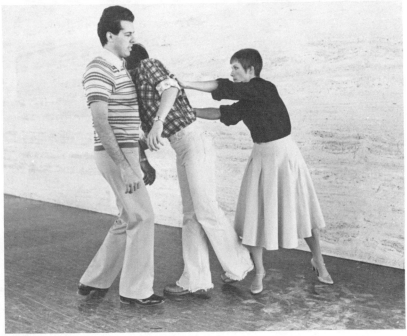

Take Action!

Try using your peripheral vision to keep both of your attackers in sight. The attacker who executes the first move is the one you have to deal with first. He will probably reach out to grab you. When he makes his move, step to the side and try to get hold of him from behind. Grab onto anything—hair, clothing, even skin. As he lunges for you, your swift move to the side will catch him off guard. Use his forward momentum to help you grab him from behind. But don't make your move until the first attacker makes his. The idea here is to catch him off balance.

Once you have him from behind, the second man will typically advance toward you to aid his partner. This is the time to use the first aggressor as your screen to block the second in his effort to grab you. Yes, this will have to be done extremely fast, and that is why it is so important to practice these techniques with your friends. After you have blocked the second man, push the first attacker into his buddy. Then, instantly, follow the number one rule of this book. Run! The brief moment in which the two villains are tangled up with each other should give you a chance to make tracks.

Do not try to be brave. This is not the occasion to use all your self-defense techniques, such as contacting the eyes and then the groin. Speed and the shift of balance are the keys to a successful escape here.

In teaching this technique to my classes, I always hear the same complaint: "I'm not that strong. In a real situation I could never do it." My response is that you do not have to be strong, because you are using your attacker's motion, his lack of balance, and the element of surprise!

If, however, you do not jump to the side at the right moment and the attacker has grabbed you or some part of your clothing, the best you can do is to apply your knee to his groin. In most cases this abrupt action will weaken him and make him loosen his grip. You can then jump to the side and follow through as described above.

Now, suppose that one attacker is holding both of your arms from behind, and the second is approaching you from the front. Wait until the second man comes into kicking range. Then, using the strong foundation of the attacker holding you from behind, lift one of your legs and kick as hard as possible into the groin of the oncoming attacker. This should delay him considerably. Plant both feet on the ground as firmly as possible. Lift your left foot and turn abruptly to the right. This should loosen your left arm. Your right arm, still being held, then works for you as a brace in keeping your balance. As

Take Action!

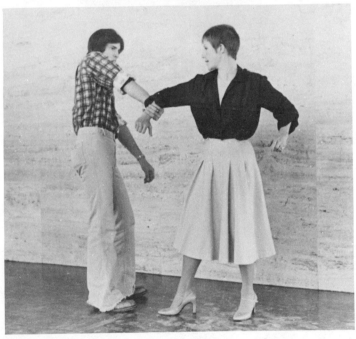

115
Take Action!

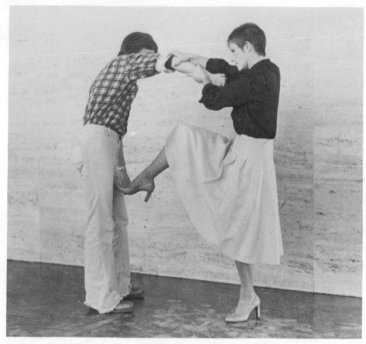

Take Action!

you turn, kick backward as hard as you can with your left foot into the groin of the man holding you. This should cause him to loosen his grip on your right arm. You are free, so don't waste a second! Turn and *run!*

But what if these maneuvers haven't worked? What if the attacker still holds on and is not discouraged by your kicking? Your move is to spin around as far as possible, slamming the heel of your free left hand into the side of his face, his ear, or his temple.

Let's summarize the situation.

The front attacker is at least slightly out of the picture after your knee or foot has struck his groin.

The rear attacker has loosened his hold on one side of your body, perhaps on both. If you've done your work right, he is knocked out of breath for a few seconds.

This should be your chance to run, but if the attacker is still able to grab you again after all this, do the following.

As you are kicking the groin of the front attacker, throw your head back into the face of the rear attacker. The crown of your head will be jammed into his face, usually striking the nose. The back of your head is hard, so it will hurt him, not you! But remember that the forward kick and the backward snap of your head must be done *simultaneously.* If the thrust is effective enough, the rear attacker will let go of you and clutch his injured nose. In case you are not completely free, try jamming your elbow into his rib cage. At the very instant the attacker's grip has loosened, turn and run!

All of this may sound complicated, but almost anyone in decent physical condition can master the necessary techniques with practice.

If you have gone through all of these steps and are still not free, you have one more chance to get away. Extend your leg sideways and, using the outside (blade area) of your foot, slam it into the attacker's knee area. Remember, it only takes about seven pounds of pressure to break or seriously injure the knee area. (Always bear this in mind when practicing any knee-breaking techniques with friendly partners!)

It is also important to remember that when you are using this technique in an actual attack, you have to keep a sharp eye on the knee area. It's small and therefore easy to miss in a split-second maneuver, and you could conceivably end up injuring your foot. Make your eyes zero in on this area as you contact it. Strikes to other body parts, such as the rib cage, can be executed pretty well without looking, since you have quite a large margin of error and there is less chance of missing your target.

After the described techniques have been applied to the rear attacker, it's time to take off. By this time, the front attacker will be ready to go again. And he will not only have recovered his strength, but will also be boiling mad. So don't wait around. Are you tired of hearing it? Run!

The two plans for countering multiple attacks that I have already described should not constitute your whole bag of tricks. Consider the following as part of your reserve arsenal.

Still using the case of two men attacking you, one from the back holding your arms and one from the front, you could choose the following strategies.

Against the front attacker:
1. Close the distance.
2. Kick him in the groin.

3. Immediately snap the foot back and bring it up in a kick to the face with the top of the foot.

Note: By recoiling your foot, you'll give your kick more impetus.

Against the rear attacker:

1. Thrust your head backward into the attacker's face. (This must be executed simultaneously with the groin kick to the front.)

2. Turn. Grab the rear attacker's head and propel your knee into his face.

3. Turn and run!

The more you practice, the more proficiency and speed you will develop. Practice will give you confidence. If you have trouble practicing the knee break against a *rear* attacker, forget it and use the following.

Move to the side of the attacker. Thrust your elbow into his rib cage or belly. Grab the back of his head. (He should be doubled over unless his stomach is made of steel.) Now thrust your knee up into his face as you are shoving his head downward. This double action is extremely effective and calls for very little energy on your part.

Once you understand how a few combinations work and have practiced them with partners, try creating your own. They should include techniques that you are comfortable with and that you feel could possibly work for you.

Stick 'Em Up! : Weapon Attacks

HANDGUNS

There are, unfortunately, many situations in which

you might be confronted with a handgun. All I can do here is describe a typical instance and make some basic suggestions for reacting.

You are accosted on the street by a man with a gun who tells you to hand over your valuables. In this example, robbery is all he has on his mind. Such robbers are usually quite nervous and don't really want to use the weapon unless they have to.

How should you react? Immediately give up whatever material belongings the gunman demands. It is better to lose your watch, your money, or any other valuables than to lose your life. You can always replace those things or get along without them.

If you resist and think you can "call his bluff," I want you to know that you may suffer serious consequences. You might anger him or increase his nervousness to the point where he does the last thing he planned: Fire the gun.

KNIVES

If you are confronted by a man with a knife, he will probably begin his attack by stalking around you, waiting and watching for what he considers will be the right time. This at least gives you a chance to establish your position, determine which hand holds the knife, and be able to maintain a safe distance. If robbery alone is the motive, immediately give up whatever the attacker demands. But if the knife-wielder is not just interested in your rings and things, don't be too eager to disrobe at his request. Try to defend yourself to the best of your ability.

The most important thing to remember in this situation is to maintain distance between you and the attacker. An attacker with a knife will almost always use a jabbing motion toward you. So follow these rules:

1. RUN (if possible).
2. If you can't run, at least maintain a safe distance. Remember, the knife is an extension of the arm.
3. When the attacker initiates a definite lunge with the knife, jump to the outside of the attacking arm. This will put you out of range, and you will also be blocking any secondary attacks he may make against you. For example, if your move to the side has caused him to lose his balance, he will start to fall forward. At that moment he could decide to make one extra jab with the knife on the way down, but you will be out of range and in a different direction.
4. If you are still unable to run, then, as you jump to the outside of the attacking arm, grab that arm with both of your hands (two is always better than one).
5. Shove the arm downward as you propel your knee upward against it. This double action of shoving his arm down while your knee comes up should loosen the attacker's hold on the weapon. Once he drops the knife, you will have a fair chance to defend yourself. Most armed attackers lose confidence as soon as the weapon is out of their hands. They have lost their security blanket, and this, of course, makes them much easier to subdue.

Don't worry about where the knife is after your attacker has been forced to drop it, unless it is right at your feet where he could easily retrieve it and use it against you. In that case, try to kick the knife out of reach. Do *not* try to pick it up and use it against him unless you are experienced in handling a knife. And I don't imagine that you practice twirling your pet knives every day. (It's probably a long time since you played mumbledy-peg.)

Now I have some sad news. If an attacker has you in a rear hold with a knife at your throat—just pray! There is absolutely nothing anyone can do in this situation. *But,* if the attacker should loosen his grip, even for a moment, you may have a chance.

Unpleasant though it is, imagine this situation: The left arm of the attacker is around your neck and his right hand has the knife at your throat.

1. Place both of your hands on his left arm. Your hands should be cupped, palms up, the fingers pointing toward your face.

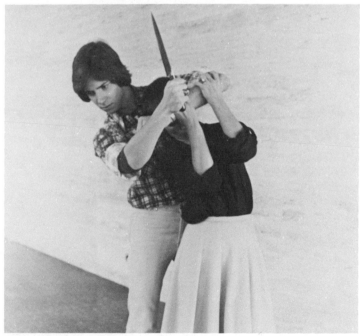

Take Action!

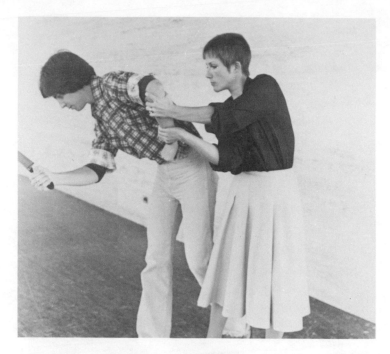

2. Simultaneously, lift your left leg and step forward and slightly out to the left side. At the same time duck your chin and push upward on the holding arm, turning your attacker away from you. This action, if performed correctly, should turn your assailant slightly to the right, so that his knife hand is being pushed away from your body.
3. Still hanging on to his left arm, position yourself behind your attacker. (This can be done only if the first part of the maneuver has been executed properly.)
4. Don't be queasy. With the right hand, grab the attacker's hair and yank as hard as possible downward as your right knee juts upward into the small of his back. (If there is little hair to pull, then grab the shirt collar or anything in that general vicinity.) This should literally sweep the attacker off his feet. When you let go of his hair (or whatever) he should end up on the ground flat on his back. Now's your chance—*Run! Run! Run!*

Please note that this must be done without any hesitation. If you pause, your attacker will either complete a turn right, loosening your hold on him, and then reattack you from the front; or will stop, reestablish his footing, and turn left, stabbing the knife into your body.

If the assailant is on the ground and it is still impossible to run, then kick and keep on kicking as hard as possible until he is incapable of doing any harm.

Here is another situation: The attacker has a knife directed straight at your chest. Your arms are above your head in a stick-up position.

1. Stay calm.
2. Create a subtle distraction. Look away and then

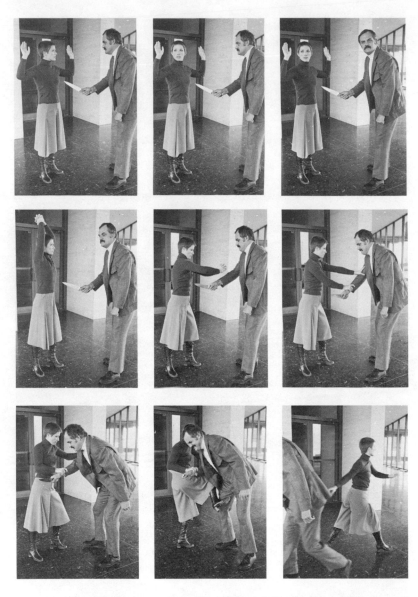

back at your attacker. If he falls for your bluff and
looks away, perform the next step immediately.
3. Clasp hands together (right hand on top) and
   overhead; slam both hands straight down on the
   knife hand of the attacker.

4. With your right hand, grab the sleeve of the hand holding the knife.
5. Moving out of the direction of the knife, grab and pull forward.
6. At the same time as number 5, propel your foot right up into his groin.
7. Run in the *opposite* direction from that in which the attacker is falling.

CLUBS OR STICKS

Up to this point, I have been advising that if you cannot run from an attacker and you have to fight it out, then maintain your distance. But this does *not* apply when someone starts swinging a rigid club or stick at you. What you must do here is focus on the arm that is holding the club. Next, believe it or not, you have to step in as close to your attacker as possible. As you step in, grab the arm that is holding the club. Remember that a club or a stick is an extension of the arm.

Once you have stepped in close, you are jamming his reach. Do not try to wrestle the club or stick out of his hand, for the average woman does not have that much power. Start kicking as hard and as fast as possible until your attacker drops his weapon and (you hope) falls to the ground. The knee repeatedly jammed into the groin is quite effective.

Suppose your attacker is using a stick or a club to hit you over the top of the head.
1. Use a crosshand block, right hand on top.
2. Step in with your left foot (we are assuming that the weapon is in the attacker's right hand).
3. With your top hand, grab the attacker's club or stick arm. Hang on, for this will help you keep your balance.
4. Simultaneously with number 3, lift your knee and

Take Action!

Take Action!

slam it into the attacker's groin. (This technique is used if you are in a medium or close position. If the distance is too far for the knee to make contact, then use your foot.)

In still another situation, your attacker has the club or stick waist-high and is intent on clobbering you on the side of the head.

In this case, you will have to depend upon your speed. As soon as he starts to strike, you have to step in close to him in order to block his use of the weapon. Frankly, I am always reluctant to recommend this type of technique because I would hate to get so close to my attacker that he might drop his weapon and wrap his arms around me in an attempt to crush me. As you surely know by now, I am a firm believer in keeping a nice far-range distance. But in these cases, you really don't have much choice. Even if he does drop his weapon and grabs you, it is still possible to escape. After all, you know a few techniques from earlier in this chapter to use in case of a held position.

CHAINS (FLEXIBLE WEAPONS)

Follow the same principles that pertain to defending yourself against a club or stick attack. The only essential difference here is that the farther around the back of your attacker you can manage to situate yourself, the better off you will be. Otherwise, the same important rule remains in this type of attack: Do not try to wrestle and overpower the weapon-holder. The main thing you must think about is to kick as hard as possible in the knee, the shin, or, if convenient, the groin. Keep on repeating this until your attacker drops his weapon and (you hope) drops himself to the ground in extreme pain. Then run!

REVIEW

Let's review the steps in a weapon attack:

1. Focus in on the weapon.
2. Note which hand the weapon is in.
3. Observe how the attacker is using the weapon (slashing, jabbing, etc.).
4. Time yourself correctly so you can leap in close to your attacker and grab the weapon arm.
5. Do not—I repeat—do not try to overpower your assailant.
6. Start kicking violently. Don't stop until the weapon *and* the attacker are on the ground. If the dropped weapon is out of retrieving range for him, forget about it. If the weapon falls at your feet, then kick it as far out of the way as possible.
7. Do not try to use the weapon unless you can confidently use it for your own good. The last thing you want is for the attacker to grab the weapon out of your hands and turn it against you.

6

SAFETY FIRST: AVOIDANCE TECHNIQUES

In this chapter we'll look at a number of potentially dangerous situations and how to handle them. It's a long list, but it encompasses cases that anyone in today's world might encounter. You don't have to be a Nervous Nellie, constantly looking over your shoulder in anticipation of an assault. Just stay alert and be prepared.

- In and Around Your Car
  - Approaching Your Car
  - Before Entering Your Car
  - Driving on City Streets
  - Parking
  - Tire Problems and What to Do
  - Protective Devices
  - Using Keys as a Weapon
- In Public Places
  - Movie Theaters
  - Public Rest Rooms
  - How to Carry a Purse or Handbag
  - Subways and Buses

- Strolling by the Lake
- When the Doorbell Rings
- Shake Hands

In and Around Your Car

APPROACHING YOUR CAR

As you approach the area where you parked the car, look around and scan the area. If you see anyone or anything that appears strange or threatening, calmly and quietly turn around and seek help.

Have the keys between the thumb and the forefinger, ready to plunge into an attacker's eyes if needed. Remember, do not hesitate, for your attacker will not. Don't be squeamish about how ugly and violent it would be to stab someone in the eyes. If you don't defend yourself, then the ugliness and the violence will be directed at *you*. The attacker doesn't care what happens to you, his victim.

In some situations you can reverse the action of the attack by being aggressive. Many times an aggressive act on your part will throw your attacker completely off base, for it will be so unexpected. Then, as soon as you have disabled your attacker, open the car door as quickly as possible, jump in, and lean with all your weight on the horn. The blasting of the horn will usually scare an attacker into fleeing the scene. If you are not blocked in tight, start the ignition and race away. And don't wait for the signal light to change. Sometimes racing through a traffic light or two will alert a police officer who will come to your assistance. (Exercise some caution, though. There's not much point in escaping an assailant only to be injured in an accident.)

BEFORE ENTERING YOUR CAR

Be sure to check the back seat for any uninvited guests. Unlock the car door and, without any wasted motion, climb in and immediately lock the door. Automatic door locks are great time-savers, but if you do not have this luxury, keep the rest of the doors locked both while the car is parked and while you are driving. Once you're in, you can relax a bit; your car is a fairly safe place.

DRIVING ON CITY STREETS

It's not always possible to know whether the neighborhood you are driving through is safe, so glance around for clues. Actually, you're better off using an expressway whenever possible. It's unlikely that with all the busy traffic on the expressway someone will pull out a gun and rob or rape you right there on the spot (although it *has* happened!).

On city streets, you are accessible to whatever loonies are around. It is not unheard of for a deranged person to take "pot shots" from an apartment window, or for someone to shoot a high-caliber rifle at you while you are waiting for a light to change.

Even barring such relatively rare occurrences, it is well to keep a few simple safety rules in mind when you are driving in the city.

Do not drive right up to the car in front of you; maintain a little distance. I would hate to become trapped in between the car in front of me and the one that is sitting on my bumper behind me! Unfortunately, this type of situation often occurs.

If you do get trapped beween two cars and you are convinced that it was done purposely, with a view to attacking you, the only thing you can do is use your car's horn. By all means, stay in the car. The worst thing you can do is get out of the car and start running; remember that you are, at least temporarily, safer inside. If your attackers start breaking the windows, push the accelerator down to the floor and smash into the car in front of you. Then place the car in reverse and once again slam the accelerator down to the floor, smashing into the car behind you. Keep repeating this, at the same time trying to turn the wheel. You may be able to squirm out, and who cares about the property damage when your life is at stake.

If situations like this seem farfetched, let me assure you that they happen every day. My best friend told me of an experience she had just recently. Ann was driving down a side street with her father and mother in the car when suddenly a teenage boy stepped in front of her car, forcing her to stop. As she looked into the rear-view mirror to see if she could back up, she saw two other boys approaching. She realized that she was blocked front and back. She motioned with her hand for the boy in front of the car to move out of the way but received only a cynical laugh in response.

Thinking fast, Ann told her parents to hang on for dear life; she was going to start the car and proceed forward. She started slowly, hoping the boy in front would become frightened and step aside, but this didn't work. She then backed up, hoping to scare the two boys behind her into moving, but this didn't work either. Now Ann realized that her only alternative was to floor the accelerator and race forward. As she did this, the boy in front of the car leaped out of her way. Without any hesitation she raced down the street ignoring traffic lights and all.

If Ann hadn't reacted the way she did, I might not have a best friend today! After everything was all over, she did admit that she was scared stiff! At the time, all she could think about was getting out of there, in no uncertain terms. Her safety and that of her loved ones came first. And that is exactly how you should think—in no uncertain terms.

PARKING

When you have no choice but to park in an unattended public parking lot, try to select a space as close as possible to the exit. And before leaving your car, glance around to check on any possibilities of trouble. If you can possibly avoid it, never park in a public underground facility when you are alone; there have been too many cases of rape, robbery, and murder in such garages for you to take such a risk. Some underground garages have electronic surveillance systems to cut down on the theft rate and to ensure their customers' safety. Nevertheless, it's better to park where real live attendants are on hand. It might cost a bit more, but your safety is worth it.

Try not to park on a side street next to an alley. Even though parking spots are scarce, it might not be a wise thing to do. An attacker could easily be crouching unseen, waiting to drag you into the alley. Don't give him the chance.

TIRE PROBLEMS AND WHAT TO DO

If your car develops a flat tire, slow down gradually and drive out of the line of traffic to the side of the highway. Look around to make sure that you are off the road, and check to see whether anyone has followed you, for many people will take advantage of a woman in trouble, given the chance.

If someone has followed you off the road, stay in your car with the doors locked and the windows tightly secured. Do not roll down the windows to talk to any stranger who pulls over to help a "maiden in distress." He may have good intentions but, on the other hand, he may not. Don't take a chance! Simply motion to him that everything is okay and thank him for stopping and offering his assistance. When the coast is clear, get out of your car and open the hood, for this is an international signal of distress. Then return to your car, relock the door, and remain there until the proper help— the police or other authorized persons—arrives.

PROTECTIVE DEVICES

There are a few devices that can help in emergencies.

Citizen band radios. Many people have citizen band radios in their cars and report to authorities when they see someone in trouble. Within a few minutes, aid should be on the way.

I have a citizen band radio in my car that I rarely use to chit-chat on, but many times I have heard calls of distress in which someone was answering and trying to help. Channel 9 is the open distress channel.

There's no need to use the C.B. radio as a regular habit, but it is good to know how to use it in case of an emergency. I know there are many drivers who abuse their federal regulation privilege but, on the other hand, there is a large percentage who do not. My inclination is to use C.B. with respect; it has saved many lives.

Alarm systems. A new mechanism called the "panic button" is now on the market, and my husband insists upon having it installed in my car. I do a lot of driving on the expressway and also in the city. If someone should try to break into my car while I'm inside, all I have to do is press a button which will set off a siren. A would-be attacker normally becomes frightened when he hears a siren, for it is signaling to the world that his intended victim is in danger and needs immediate assistance. Many people who are unwilling to become physically involved when someone is in trouble are ready to help behind the scenes by telephoning to the proper authorities.

There is another new car emergency device which seems unusual but is very effective. Hooked up, let us say, to my car, this system is activated when the car is being broken into. A siren goes off for the count of three, and then my previously taped voice screams: "HELP! HELP! THEY'RE TRYING TO STEAL ME AND I'M THE PROPERTY OF KATHY BURG." This message would be repeated until I am notified and come to the scene to shut off the alarm. The same system can also be wired to the gas tank, so that the alarm will be triggered when someone attempts to steal your gas supply.

This is a great gimmick, but it will be some time before it is widely available. Keep watching for it.

USING KEYS AS A WEAPON

Keys may come in handy not only when you approach your car, but also when you are walking down the street or entering your apartment or home. The jagged edges of your keys can be held between the thumb and the forefinger, ready to be poked into someone's eyes if necessary.

When you are in an elevator going to your apartment floor, it is a very good idea to have your keys in hand just in case someone is lurking in the hallway and up to no good. If this does happen, you will have your keys ready, as you make a quick dash for your apartment, so that you will be able to open your door and quickly enter into safety.

If you live in a house, be sure to glance at the front door and also up and down the street before you leave your car. You should also have your keys ready here. If you see anyone—or anything—that seems a little suspicious or unusual, do not leave your car. Stay inside and wait for someone you know—husband, friend, neighbor—to arrive. Otherwise, start the engine and drive to where you can obtain help. The police can check out the area and also escort you to your home. Make sure everything is all right outside and inside of the house before they leave. Always take heed of your intuition. If you feel something is not quite right, then don't take a chance. It is better to be embarrassed (even though you shouldn't be) than injured or dead. Never be afraid to tell someone that you are frightened; very few of us have the courage of Joan of Arc when facing danger.

In Public Places

MOVIE THEATERS

I really enjoy attending movies, but I have learned to be extremely careful when I am not with my husband. If you go to a movie by yourself, be ready to take extra precautions. Once you are in the theater door, be sure to glance around and make sure no one is looking at you with special interest. After you have entered the dark auditorium, stand in the rear with your back to the wall until your eyes have adjusted. Then select your seat with care. Look around to see who will be sitting near you (this means in front, in back, and to both sides). I usually try to choose the middle of the theater where there

Safety First: Avoidance Techniques

are quite a few people. Never sit right next to a stranger in a relatively empty row. It's best to sit in a populated area, but three to four seats away from others. If you notice anyone staring at you, get up and leave. A person staring at you is not interested in the movie!

If, after you are seated, someone gets up and moves toward you, without hesitation get up and leave. When you go to a movie alone, you are taking the chance of having to miss the happy ending. But it's better to leave than risk your own unhappy ending!

Now, please understand something. Just because I'm warning you about going to the movies alone doesn't mean that your safety is guaranteed if you have a companion. Offenders with robbery in mind will often work in teams, especially when they are planning to attack a couple. Situations have been reported in which a couple seated in a theater have had one assailant move in next to them and the other situate himself so as to block the exit. The attacker seated next to the couple then would initiate the first attack. The couple would try to escape, but the second attacker would block the escape route. This system seems quite popular with certain criminals. It is easier to operate with a buddy around, just in case something backfires. Even though being with someone doesn't make you immune to attack, it is nevertheless safer to be accompanied by another person, male or female. Many attackers will hesitate to take on two (or more) people, although some just don't care. Not all criminals are intelligent, problem-solving individuals!

Most women carry purses and/or shopping bags into a theater. In some theaters, a reel comes on warning women not to leave their bags or other be-

Safety First: Avoidance Techniques

longings on the seat next to them or on the floor. Well, I've heard many people laugh at this warning, but I'll bet they won't laugh when their purses are stolen.

Another tip to consider: If your companion decides to venture into the lobby to buy popcorn, go with him or her. It might turn out to be fun, and it's certainly safer.

PUBLIC REST ROOMS

Sometimes potential attackers lurk around public facilities such as ladies' rooms, where they hope to catch someone alone and unguarded. If you are with a male companion and need to use such facilities, be sure to have your companion wait outside the door. By previous arrangement, if a certain length of time has elapsed and you have not emerged, your companion should seek the management's help. And if that doesn't work, he should just walk in. Better to have a few embarrassed women to contend with than someone holding a knife to your throat without fear of intervention.

HOW TO CARRY A PURSE OR HANDBAG

When walking through a crowd, you are looking for trouble if you let your purse dangle at your side with the latch facing outward. This is like a formal invitation even to an inexperienced pickpocket, let alone a purse-snatcher. Slip your arm through the strap, with your hand under the bottom of the purse, and then clutch it firmly under your arm. If the purse has no strap, then hold it tight against your chest. If you insist on carrying an open handbag, at least make sure you have everything of value on the bottom and items of lesser value toward the open top.

Always consider security when purchasing a

purse. For everyday use, look for double handles and firm clasps or zippered tops. A large bag or tote that you take to the beach can be open, since it probably won't contain anything of great value. The loss of a beach towel or a pair of sunglasses obviously won't make a big dent in your life.

Subways and Buses

Those who use public transportation to get to and from work often have to endure a long, uncomfortable ride in a train or bus packed with bodies. Aside from the unpleasantness of such a trip, passengers may be prey to pickpockets or, if they are women, to strangers who can't keep their hands to themselves. Of course, the ideal solution is to avoid the mad rush hours altogether by adjusting your working time so that you leave home a little later in the morning and work a little later in the evening. But perhaps you have no choice about when to travel. In that case you may one day find yourself in a situation where you need to use a technique from this book.

Here, as in all such situations, the key to the problem is common sense. Suppose you're in a crowded bus where everyone is sandwiched in, and the guy breathing down your neck decides to check out your body. If you really can't move, then it would be foolish to fight back and perhaps aggravate the offender into doing something worse. Don't forget that whenever you use physical action to defend yourself, *you must have an escape route*. Otherwise you are placing yourself in more danger than when you started out. In this example, the best thing to do is simply get off at the next stop and wait for another bus to come along.

Let's say you do have a way to escape. Then you can use the back of your head to smash into the offender's face, chin, or throat. If you have a little room to move your limbs, you can use your elbow to strike his rib cage. Or you could stomp on his instep.

These are just a few examples of sensible ways to react. The more you practice the basic techniques taught in the previous chapters, the more readily you will be able to apply them to various situations. It's also good to do some mental practice by thinking up possible situations and figuring out how you would respond according to the knowledge you've gained through your practice.

Strolling by the Lake

Sounds lovely, doesn't it? But what if you are walking down by a lakefront in a city like Chicago and someone attacks you? If you're a good swimmer (and it's not midwinter), your best escape route might be the water. Jump in and swim underneath the surface as far out as possible. Your attacker will probably not be willing to go so far as to dive in after you. In the water, you'll have a far better chance of survival than on dry land. Be sure to stay underwater as long as possible. When you do have to surface, try to come up just enough to obtain sufficient air for you to go under again. Never mind looking around to see where your attacker is; he just might have a gun and be waiting for you to reappear. The last thing an attacker wants is for his victim to be able to identify him.

But maybe you're not a mermaid and a jump in the lake (or ocean) doesn't appeal to you. Play it safe. Select areas that are well guarded by the police, and pick a strolling time when you won't be isolated. Central Park in New York, the lakefront in Chicago, or the wharf area in San Francisco are beautiful places to visit, but be careful; criminals make it their business to take advantage of the tourist's naiveté.

When the Doorbell Rings

Many people have been attacked in their own homes because they were tricked into opening the door to their attackers. So it's always wise to be cautious when someone rings your bell—even if you are expecting a delivery or a guest.

A bit of acting often helps when someone is at the door. Here's one of my own acts. I have a Red Lored Amazon Parrot named Ding-a-ling who looks ferocious but is really quite tame. When I was living alone, every time I had anything delivered to my apartment, I placed Ding-a-ling on my shoulder before answering the door. The delivery man would usually say, "What a pretty little bird," or some such comment. I would immediately warn him in grave tones that he'd better stand back, as the parrot was vicious and had a tendency to attack strangers. Result: Many a pizza was slid along the floor to my apartment door from a "safe" distance, and many a payment was tossed out. I would then immediately lock the door and laugh. If they only knew how harmless the bird really was!

So you see, acting and a little common sense go a long way. You might have fun inventing your own techniques for different circumstances. Try it and see just how clever you can be.

The "Invisible Man" routine is another act I

dreamed up for use in case of trouble. When a delivery man or other stranger rings the doorbell, have the radio on in the next room. On your way to the door, shout out to your invisible man that you will see who's there and that he need not bother. After you have opened the door, once again call out to your invisible man, telling him who is at the door and that you will take care of it and be right back. This works like a charm.

Incidentally, don't assume that you're perfectly safe if the stranger at your door is a woman. She could be part of a team of robbers, and her buddies may be waiting just out of sight. If you have any doubt about the person at your door, simply refuse to open it. If the caller is making a delivery, instruct him to leave it in the hall or on the front steps. Should he refuse, then say that you just stepped out of the shower and cannot possibly open the door and that your husband is sleeping and you have no intention of waking him. If the caller again refuses, tell him to take whatever he is delivering and return tomorrow. Be sure to specify a time when you know someone will be home with you.

Once the door is open, you are lessening the degree of safety that you should maintain. Nothing is so important that it cannot wait until the next day, especially when your safety is in question. I can't repeat too often that material objects can be replaced, but your life cannot!

Shake Hands

It may sound incredible, but there are some men who will try to cause physical harm to you in front of others. I have seen this happen on numerous occasions. It typically occurs during a handshake. This species of "hearty" handshaker enjoys belittling women. He wants to demonstrate that they are not only weaker but also subservient. And, sure enough, after a few seconds in his grip you will be bent over from the pain, and thus slightly lower than your normal level. In other words, you are in a bowing position, and your handshaker enjoys this!

If someone grabs your hand and squeezes it so tight that you feel as if it will fall off your wrist when he lets go, follow these steps:

1. Try to squeeze back. This might startle him for a brief moment, allowing you to withdraw your hand.
2. If step 1 doesn't work and instead of letting go, he starts to squeeze harder, bend your knees and slightly collapse, to show how painful his grasp is.
3. Along with step 2, a slight screech of pain would help. Other people standing around will probably come to your aid, especially men. The Age of Chivalry may be dead, but most men still hate to see a woman treated in a brutal way.

Should these steps fail, it's time to unsheathe the weapon you always have at hand (unless you still bite your nails!). Dig the nails of your free hand down into his skin. Don't worry if you draw blood; after all, it's a few drops of his blood against your mangled hand. Keep calm. While your nails are doing their work, be sure to look him straight in the eyes to show him that you mean business.

Finally, if he is still trying to play Charlie Atlas and your pain is becoming unbearable, then kick him as hard as possible in the shins. I guarantee that he will let go, and he'll probably walk—or hobble—away immediately.

Safety First: Avoidance Techniques

7

SHAPE UP OR SHIP OUT: DAILY EXERCISES

A Simple Program of Daily Exercises

We all know that the ideal way to stay in top physical condition is to work out for a couple of hours a day every day of the week. But who else besides the competitive athlete or the determined sports enthusiast really has the time and the ambition?

Now, I'm not going to kid you. To be able to defend yourself with the maneuvers described in the preceding chapters, you must be in proper shape to meet your own bodily needs. And to achieve that, all you really need is to exert yourself physically three times a week. That will do the job in the staying-in-shape department. But even better is to try to exert yourself at least once a day. The ideal conditioning program is to exercise fifteen minutes in the morning and fifteen minutes before retiring at night.

The program I am about to suggest works for me,

and I am the kind of person who would rather sleep ten minutes longer than get up and go through a forty-five- or fifty-minute regimen. Exercising for only fifteen minutes in the morning lets me get those few extra minutes of sleep and does not tire me out for the rest of the day. On the contrary, it warms up my motor so I am ready for the day ahead of me.

The exercises given here are geared not to build up huge muscles but rather to keep you in overall tiptop shape. The program includes:
• Easy stretching
• Isometrics
• Breathing and relaxing techniques
• Cardiovascular builders (to improve your pulse rate)

As you well know, my system of womanly self-defense relies heavily on the basic technique of running. If you are out of breath after ten yards and your muscles are complaining to your brain that they hurt and cannot keep going, then what's the use of even trying to learn this system?

Morning Routine—Fifteen Minutes

When you wake up in the morning, just remain in a nice relaxed position for at least five minutes. While lying in this position, concentrate on your breathing. When you feel you are fully relaxed, think over the day's itinerary. Now rise. First, take a nice deep breath, filling your lungs to the brim with oxygen. Then exhale by pushing the air all the way out and down through the chest, until you have a nice, tight abdomen.

Now you're ready to follow these simple steps to a well-conditioned, healthier body.

After sitting up in bed:

1. Swing both your legs over the side of the bed.
2. Stretch both arms up over your head.
3. Look up toward the ceiling.
4. Make a large circle with the arms while pushing the chest outward.

Now stand up.

1. Stretch the arms up over the head with the feeling that you can almost touch the ceiling.
2. Then collapse all the way down to the floor in a "Raggedy Ann" position. Repeat steps 1 and 2 three times.
3. Rotate the neck in one direction, then reverse and rotate in the other direction. Repeat three times in each direction.
4. Rotate the shoulder blades backward and then forward. Then rotate one shoulder at a time. First roll the right shoulder forward and then the left. (Repeat the same procedure, reversing the direction. Rotate three times in each direction.)
5. Extend the arms overhead and clasp the hands together. Stretch up toward the ceiling, release the hands, and move the arms backward and downward in a circular motion until they are below the buttocks. Reclasp the hands behind the back and stretch forward by bending from the waist. Straighten up.
6. Place the right leg behind the left, bend the knees, and—without the aid of the hands—lower yourself to the floor.
7. Bring both knees up to the chest and hug the knees by pulling them into the chest. Make sure

Shape Up or Ship Out: Daily Exercises

that your head is bent forward so you will have a complete stretch from the top of the spine all the way down to the bottom. This stretch feels fantastic and is good for the back muscles.

8. From this seated position, still holding the knees, roll backward and forward. This roll should take you back onto the shoulders and then up into a sitting position. This is a great massage for the buttocks and also a greater stretcher for the spine.

9. Try to roll on the third count all the way up into a shoulder stand. (Another name for this position is the "bicycle stand.") Hold this for a count of three, then slowly roll back down without the use of your hands and stretch the legs straight out in front of you.

10. Lying flat on your back, tighten the tummy (abdominal) muscles. Hold for three seconds. Relax and repeat three times.

Note: Be sure to push the small of your back down into the floor as you tighten the abdominal muscles.

11. Lying on your back, lift both legs only eight inches off the floor. Hold three seconds. Lower the legs back down onto the floor at the same time that you are pushing the small of your back down. Repeat three times.

12. From your back, roll over until you are facing downward. Push up onto your knees.

Note: Never kneel on the floor without some type of protective padding beneath you, since the knees have a protective layer of fat to cushion them.

Shape Up or Ship Out: Daily Exercises

Keep your hands on the floor in a catlike position. Slide your arms out in front of you and try to lower your nose to the floor by bending the elbows. Remember to keep your back as straight as possible. Do not let your lower back sway or sag, for this will cause discomfort later on in the day—or even in later life. Straighten the elbows and look

Shape Up or Ship Out: Daily Exercises

straight ahead. Lift the head up to look at the ceiling and stretch the neck muscles. Open and close your mouth. This exercise is superb for:
- building strength in your upper body
- stretching and relaxing the neck and facial muscles
- firming the breasts
13. Still in the kneeling position, lower the forehead to the floor. Let the arms relax out at the sides, and sit back on your legs. Hold this position for ten seconds and concentrate on your breathing or on some pleasant thought.
14. Rise slowly, one vertebra at a time.
15. Stand. . . . Smile. . . . Tell yourself how great you feel and how wonderful this day is going to be.

Being in good shape refers not only to the body but also to the mind. If you wake up in the morning feeling tired and unenthusiastic about the day ahead, and if you dwell on these feelings over and over again in your mind, you will eventually convince yourself that you really do feel miserable. Feeling sorry for yourself might make you weaken and crawl back into bed to hide underneath the covers.

Don't let your weaknesses get the best of you. Tell yourself how great you feel, and after a few minutes you will! Sometimes, after my husband and I have entertained friends until the wee hours, I'm not exactly in the mood to "rise and shine" in the morning. But if I go right into my exercise program and keep busily moving, it stimulates my system and gives me the energy—and optimism—I need to get me through the day.

Shape Up or Ship Out: Daily Exercises

CONDENSED REVIEW OF THE MORNING EXERCISE ROUTINE

This review will make it easy to remember your exercises by memorizing key words.

1. Wake up, breathe, and think of your day ahead.
2. Sit up and stretch.
3. Stand and stretch up overhead.
4. Neck rotations.
5. Shoulder rotations.
6. Arms overhead and stretch upward, circle arms below buttocks, and bend forward.
7. Sit on floor.
8. Hug knees and rock back and forth.
9. Shoulder stand.
10. Tummy tighteners.
11. Leg lifts.
12. Roll over and do semi-push-ups.
13. Relax
14. Rise.
15. Stand . . . smile . . . and tell yourself how great you feel.

Evening Routine—Fifteen Minutes

The evening exercises are not too strenuous, because that might cause you to be tense rather than relaxed. Instead, they consist of stretching out the muscles, toning and relaxing them at the same time.

These exercises should be done just before going to bed. Once you have it down properly, you can expect two bonus benefits—aid in preventing insomnia, and stimulation of the body fluids that help break down carbohydrates, fats, and other nutrients while you are asleep.

Isn't it a happy thought that after you are in never-never land your body is still working for you? You could almost say that it is exercising for you while you are unconscious. This should appeal to those of us who are quite lazy when it comes to actually working out in a daily exercise program and who also like all the munchies at the dinner table.

I do have one cautionary note here. Just because some of the body's functions are automatic, it is often referred to as a "machine." This is misleading because you can't turn its various parts on and off like a motor. What if your heart "turned off" for a few minutes? 'Nuff said!

Now to the exercises themselves. Since these are meant to be relaxing, do them with a nice, easy tempo.

STRETCHES

1. While standing, stretch the arms up overhead. Inhale as you stretch the arms upward and then hold your breath for a count of ten. As you drop your arms, exhale by blowing all the air out of the lungs. Repeat three times. Drop down into a squatting position and then rise, one vertebra at a time.

2. Stand. Bend your elbows and hold them chest-high in front of you. Spread your feet shoulder-width apart. With the feet firmly planted, turn to the right and look over your right shoulder, then to your left. Repeat ten times.

Value: Excellent for the waistline and also for the relaxation of the lower back.

3. Extend the arms straight in front of the body at shoulder height. Swing them backward and clap the hands together behind the body. Then swing

Shape Up or Ship Out: Daily Exercises

the arms forward and clap the hands in front of the body. Repeat ten times.

Value: Good for stretching out the chest and for relaxing the upper shoulder area.

4. Roll the shoulders forward and then backward; alternate shoulders. Repeat three times.

Value: Relaxation of the shoulder area, where tension is usually concentrated.

5. Extend the right arm straight up overhead. Keep the left arm down at your side. With the body facing forward, stretch toward the left. As you stretch, reach over with the extended right arm as if you were trying to touch the floor on the left side. Let the left arm slide down the body, trying to touch the floor. Repeat with the left arm overhead. Repeat ten times each side.

6. Drop down and sit with the legs stretched as far apart as possible. Stretch the body by reaching to touch the toes of one foot with the fingertips of both hands. Then stretch toward the other foot. Repeat three times each side:

With the toes pointed
With the foot flexed
Alternating pointed toe and flexed foot

Example:
3 pointed stretches to the right
3 pointed stretches to the left
3 flexed stretches to the left
3 flexed stretches to the right

Value: Stretches the hamstring muscles (in the back of the legs) when the foot is in a flexed position. Stretches the upper front muscles of the legs when the foot is in a pointed position.

7. Sit with both legs pulled up, knees bent, heels together, hands on ankles. Push both the knees down with the hands and try to touch the knees to the floor and hold for three counts. Repeat three times.
8. Hug the knees to the chest. Hold for three counts, then relax. Be sure to drop your head forward so you get a good spinal pull from the top of your head down to your tailbone.
9. Roll up onto the shoulders in a bicycle position and pedal for a count of twenty. Remember, keep the tempo nice and easy.
10. Roll down gradually by placing one vertebra on the floor at a time. Stretch the legs straight out in front of you as you push the small of the back into the floor. Relax.

Value: Improves circulation; helps prevent varicose veins; bathes brain cells.

SIT-UPS

Be sure that you do your sit-ups in a "hook line position." This means your knees should be bent and your feet flat on the floor. Straight-leg sit-ups are *not* recommended, because they can strain your back. Sit-ups will help flatten the tummy. And if you're worried about developing a muscular bulge, forget it; you'd have to do quite a few to get to that point. For a flat tummy, keep the sit-ups to a number you feel comfortable with. If you do want a muscular, athletic look, increase the number of sit-ups to the point where you really feel that you are pushing yourself.

Beginner sit-ups
1. Sit on the floor, with knees bent and feet flat on floor.

2. Cup knees with hands.
3. Roll backward until you are lying flat on your back. Your knees are still up and your feet on the floor.
4. Slide hands down the body until they are resting at your sides.
5. Rise back up to a sitting position. If you are having trouble on the way up, grab the knees to maintain your balance and help pull you up.

Advanced Sit-ups. When you have mastered the beginner sit-ups, move on to the following advanced variations:
1. Sit up without using the hands to balance.
2. Sit up with hands on the tummy.
3. Sit up with hands behind the head.
4. With hands behind your head, lean forward after each sit-up and try to touch the floor with your forehead.
5. For the really advanced "sitter-upper": Sit up without using your hands. Feet are about three inches off the floor. As you sit up, touch the toes. As you lie back, stretch the legs out. Do not let the feet touch the floor. Notice that when you sit up, you will be balancing on your tailbone. Be sure to stretch up nice and tall!

After you have completed your sit-ups, roll over and curl up in the embryonic position. Remain for about a count of ten, then slowly stretch out until you are lying flat on your back.

RELAXATION
This is the last step before you snuggle down for the night. In fact, you can do it in bed.
1. Lie on your back, feet slightly apart, hands lazily at your sides with palms facing upward.

2. Inhale through the nose. Exhale through the mouth (concentrate on the breathing).

3. Tense a body part and then relax it.

Concentrate on each area as you tense up. Follow the sequence listed below. You should feel a heavy, tingling sensation when you relax that specific body segment.

- Left foot
- Right foot
- Right knee
- Left knee
- Right thigh
- Left thigh
- Right buttock
- Left buttock
- Abdominal area
- Chest
- Right hand
- Left hand
- Right arm
- Left arm
- Right shoulder
- Left shoulder
- Neck
- Facial muscles

4. Finally, tense up the entire body all at once. Relax!

Running

In addition to the morning and evening exercise routines, you should fit in a running program at least three times a week. It isn't difficult to fit your running practice in if you plan ahead and insist upon your body performing. After you've finished, you'll

Shape Up or Ship Out: Daily Exercises

feel great, so don't listen to that little voice in your head that keeps urging you to go lie down instead. Resist the temptation, and the sooner you start moving the sooner you will be finished.

Before running, take a few minutes and stretch out the muscles. It's easy.
1. Shake out all your muscles:
   • Legs
   • Arms
   • Hands
   • Feet
   • Neck
2. Take five easy jumps. Do not exert any energy, just loosen up the ankle joints.
3. Breathe deeply, hold, and exhale. Repeat several times.
4. Lunge right and hold three seconds. Make sure your knee is aligned straight over your toes; this is very important. Repeat to the left side.
5. Sit on the ground in the hurdler's position.

Hurdler's Position:
a. Sit on the ground with the right leg extended straight out in front of the body.
b. Left leg is in a bent position behind the body. Your knee will be facing outward and your left ankle will almost be touching your derriere.
   Lean over and place chest on one knee, hold three counts. Do the same on the other side. Repeat five times each side.

   Value: This exercise will stretch the hamstring muscles, which you need for running.
6. Remain seated, with the legs together. Lean forward and try to place your forehead on your

Shape Up or Ship Out: Daily Exercises

knees, fingers touching the toes. Stretch down and hold for three counts. Repeat three times.

7. Stand up and start an easy jogging in place. Remember to breathe deeply and shake all the upper muscles loose.

POSTSCRIPT

If You Want to Learn More . . .

After reading about my system of womanly self-defense, maybe some of you are still saying, "It's a good idea, but I could never build up the aggressive attitude that it takes in time of danger." Perhaps you feel you need to develop a little more natural aggression without jeopardizing your own sense of femininity. One way to do that is to take up fencing.

While teaching French foil fencing to women at a small college, I discovered that in the first five weeks of class, many of the students would hold back and let their opponents make the initial attack. But under my constant prodding and urging them to attack, the natural aggressive attitudes started to emerge. Certain students who I thought would never say "Boo!" started on the attack and became winners when they competed.

After a survey of several of my fencing classes, I concluded that the reason students registered for this specific class was that they wanted to learn some type of sport that could help them to defend themselves in case of attack. The general opinion of the class was that they would be learning how to use a weapon in a respectable and safe way.

Many of the students did not realize that in learning how to fence they would also be developing:
• Body coordination
• Agility
• Hand-eye coordination
• Endurance
• Speed
• Reflex actions
• Natural aggression

Many of the students were extremely proud of themselves. They lost a few pounds, toned up their muscles, and had fun at the same time. This might be the best way to indoctrinate yourself gradually. Ease into the idea of defending yourself a little at a time.

In the last weeks of one of my classes, I noticed that the students were proudly carrying their French foils around campus. I also noticed a few of the students carrying umbrellas (same principle as a foil), knowing they could use them to help maintain a distance from an attacker, or even to jab him where it hurts. I myself carry an umbrella with a sharp point on the end. After all, I never know when I might have to use it to maintain distance or even to parry (a fencing term meaning to block an attack) a knife that is being thrust in my direction. It is almost like a security blanket, or a vote of confidence in my ability to use my fencing techniques even when I am walking down the street instead of working out in the gym. If Errol Flynn could see me now!

After you have taken a fencing course and you would like to make even more progress, try signing up at the Y or some community center that offers a course in self-defense. Most likely, you will be the most advanced student in the class since fencing will have taught you how to move, react, and think in time of danger.

Now, if you would like to dedicate still more time to your own protection, it might be a good idea to consider taking a class at a school of martial arts— bearing in mind the comments made in Chapter 1 about such courses. It might—or might not—be your cup of tea. In any case, be sure to observe a few classes before you sign any contracts with a school.

A Special Note for Mothers

Once you have had enough practice with the moves taught in this book, you might consider teaching your children a few simple self-defense techniques. Assaults against children by adults—including sexual abuse and kidnaping—are not only common; they are actually increasing. Moreover, there is the possibility that your child might be threatened in some way by older, bigger children.

Teaching your child a few techniques will make you feel more secure about their safety, since you will know that they can defend themselves to some extent. Of course, in some situations, a child will be powerless to fight back. But in many others, she or he may well be able to escape unharmed.

In addition, self-defense lessons for children will:
• Develop and improve their thinking processes
• Develop and improve their coordination, agility, and speed
• Develop their muscle tone

Finally, by teaching your children, you yourself will become more proficient. If you are able to teach a technique to someone else, that means you understand it thoroughly.

Before you instruct children in self-defense, make sure they understand two basic points:

1. *Common sense must be used in daily life.* Teach your children the commonsense rules of how to avoid trouble and, if you remind them often enough, they'll make a habit of following those rules. Commonsense caution and self-defense methods will come as naturally to them as the observation of everyday safety rules—such as looking both ways before crossing the street.

2. *Self-defense techniques must only be used in certain appropriate situations.* In other words, children must understand when to use physical tactics and when not to use them. For example, they must realize that they are *not* to use their newly learned knowledge against friends in a play situation.

Words of Wisdom

I hope you've learned some useful tips on how to defend yourself. Just remember, though, that all the book knowledge you've absorbed won't help you unless you *practice* what I've preached.

Every once in a while, skim through this book and

review the basic areas and your favorite techniques so that they become second nature. Strong basic moves will ensure your success.

My sincerest wish is that you will never have to make use of what you learned here. But if you do, just be sure to stay calm and use your controlled anger to your best advantage.

Stay in shape!

Remain confident!

Use your common sense!